best wishes Duane

AROUND
THE ROCK IN A BAD MOOD
BY
BERNIE HOWGATE

fond memories of the Rock
go for it

Bernie Howgate

The Travelling Man
Enterprises

WEBSITE
www.berniehowgate.com
Email
berniehowgate@hotmail.com

AROUND THE ROCK IN A BAD MOOD
First Edition

WRITTEN
Bernie Howgate

Edited
Wendy Reger

COVER MAPS AND ILLUSTRATIONS
Bernie Howgate and Wendy Reger

PHOTOGRAPHS
Bernie Howgate and Newfoundland Tourism

PUBLISHED
The Travelling Man Enterprises
General Delivery
Mud Lake
Labrador
A0P 1K0

FIRST EDITION
2006
Printed in Canada
ISBN-0-9694419-3-2
COPYRIGHT@BERNIE HOWGATE

Something inexplicable happens when a man picks up a tool to do some home repairs. Some force, as yet undescribed by science, but nevertheless well known to women, is set loose. It's a force that lures men away from their families and the things they are supposed to be doing to the place where hammers are being swung
Maybe the act of a hammer moving through the air sets off a cosmic thrumming only men can hear. Or maybe when a man picks up a screwdriver, he releases an odour only men with tools can smell - a musty, yeasty sort of smell, with a hint of leather and WD40. Men in their backyards racking leaves and men in their basements listening to ball games on portable radios are seized by this odour the way the urge to migrate seizes lesser species. Suddenly they're thinking, I don't belong here anymore. I belong in another place. I should be doing something else, and I should take my axe with me just in case.

Stuart Mclean

Books in Print

Tales of a Travelling man:
based on an eight year round the world cycle trip
ISBN-0-9694419-0-8
$30:00 postage included

Journey through Labrador:
based on an eight month snowshoe and sea kayaking trip up the Labrador coast
ISBN-0-9694419-1-6
$25:00 postage included

Newfie or Bust :
based on an eight month 9000km cycle trip across Canada from Victoria, British Columbia to St John's, Newfoundland
ISBN-0-9694419-2-4
$25:00 postage included

Lazy Days in Summer:
based on a 4500km sea kayaking trip from the Great Lakes down the Saint Lawrence river to Goose Bay, Labrador
ISBN-0-9694419-4-0
$25:00 postage included

Contact: for book purchase

Bernie Howgate's Home Page:
http//.www.berniehowgate.com

Email:

berniehowgate@hotmail.com

Snail mail:
Bernie Howgate, c/o Travelling Man Enterprises, Mud Lake, Labrador, A0P 1K0, CANADA

to my dear friends in Sept-Îles

**Denis Jean & Germaine Carrier, J.P & Danielle
Uncle George & 'pretty boy' William,
Jean & Renée-Claude
Mo Jo & Emily
not forgetting Hector Blake**

**thanks a million
for your patience and support**

Contents

1: The Rock   page 1
2: Life is Delicious   20
3: The Southern Shore   27
4: Popeye the Sailor Man   36
5: Primary Colours   42
6: No Pain, No Gain   49
7: Lean, Mean, Paddling Machine   56
8: Coming Home   64
9: Brutal Weather but Fantastic Hospitality   71
10: Where have all the Lighthouses gone?   82
11: Good Golly Miss Molly   91
12: A Diamond in the Rock called St. John's   96
13: Seas within a Sea   106
14: Sea of Haze   115
15: Family Tradition   124
16: Notre Dame Bay   131
17: Fog-Fog-Fog   144
18: Beware of the Clear Days   159
19: Strait of Belle Isle   165
20: Gulf of St. Lawrence   172
21: Long Range Mountains   180
22: What goes around comes around   186
23: Welcome Home   192

Map Illustrations

1: Corner Brook to Grand Bruit   page 3
2: Grand Bruit to McCallum   26
3: McCallum to Argentia   48
4: Argentia to St. John's   70
5: St. John's to Bonavista   95
6: Bonavista to Musgrave Harbour   114
7: Musgrave Harbour to Beaumont   130
8: Beaumont to Harbour Deep   143
9: Harbour Deep to Bird Cove   150
10: Bird Cove to Corner Brook   171

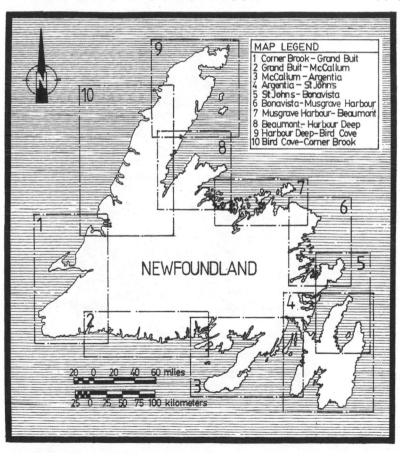

A sailor's geography is not always that of the cartographer, for whom a cape is a cape, with a latitude and longitude. For the sailor, a great cape is both a very simple an extremely complicated whole of rocks, currents, breaking seas and huge waves, fair winds and gales, joys and fears, fatigue, dreams, painful hands, empty stomachs, wonderful moments, and suffering.

Bernard Moitessier

Chapter: 1
The Rock

Yes, I am back in the saddle again. Maybe; I am over 50 years old. Maybe I should slow down, paddle in warmer waters; but who wants to be "Smiley Grey?" I search for discord, not harmony and trust pain over pleasure. The cold suits my character, and the rocks that Newfoundland is built on stand for stability in my eyes. I love the freedom and endless horizons that ocean travel afford me, and I find its sweet scented breezes invigorating. Meeting people has always been the name of the game when I travel, and I now looked forward to all that Newfoundland has to offer.

I remember as if it was yesterday seeing a map of Newfoundland for the first time. Community names jumped out and splashed my eyes in vivid brushstrokes of primary colour. Take for instance, Sally's Cove; I wonder what she did to deserve such a name. L'anse Amour, Maiden Arm, Fortune Bay, Tickle Harbour, Ho Ho Bay, Heart's Desire; and I'd not even scratched the surface. None of these names owed anything to tradition. These were the creations of men ruled by emotion, with strong ties to land and relationships; but not all community names suggest one's brighter side. You only have to see Deadman's Bay to read into Newfoundland's darker passions as well as its grim humour; Wreck Cove, Wild Blight, Blow Me Down and Jerry's Nose; no other places in the world have constantly suggested these fundamental human emotions and imprinted them on their community names. While those names had put fire in my belly then, my first day of ocean kayaking would fanned its embers into a roaring inferno.

"How's it going Bernie?"

Bob sat at the kitchen table, armed and ready with a glass of wine. I had met Bob Diamond six years earlier in Goose Bay, Labrador. Ex RCMP, Environmentalist, and family man, Bob's one of those gentle giants with a mop of curly hair and a smile as warm as a furnace. He's a Newfoundlander through and through. Salt sea air flows through his veins as naturally as blood. The word hospitality to him, like many Newfoundlanders, isn't just a word it's a way of life. We'd met years before and parted on a loose invitation, "If you're ever down my way......" and now six years later, I am sitting down at his kitchen table feasting on pizza and drinking glasses of his homemade wine. That night, one bottle stretched into two. The conversation was lively and full of back-slapping optimism, and the last I remember, his wife Mary was reminding me where the bedroom was. I was drunk as a skunk.

I woke up the next morning feeling like I was on death row, but as soon as the crisp morning air had slapped me, I was raring to go. I believe sometimes, that I can see beyond the present and see quick shots of coming events, as if loose brain wires briefly connected. It's frightening to think you're only one step away from the insane asylum, but the solo voyageur is a superstitious animal. Some of us carry good luck charms or letters of encouragement on our trips. I had even heard of a man who soloed the arctic with a pair of his wife's panties in his pocket. I am neither that romantic nor that superstitious. I treat the first day as the last. My mantra is, "what goes around, comes around." If the first day goes smoothly, so will the last. I treat them all like bookends. The space between is the story, the icing on the cake.

It was something that Bob had said as we parted that morning, that gave me the uplift I was looking for. It wasn't so much his words of encouragement, the ones that friends often offer each other during moments of challenge. It was the emphasis he placed on, "See you back here in four months." Those words instantly rang like church bells in my ears. We are all mortal. It seems, some of us more than others, so how much sweeter life becomes with the certain knowledge that you've cheated the devil, if only for four months. It's like being given permission to be a child again, but that feeling didn't last long.

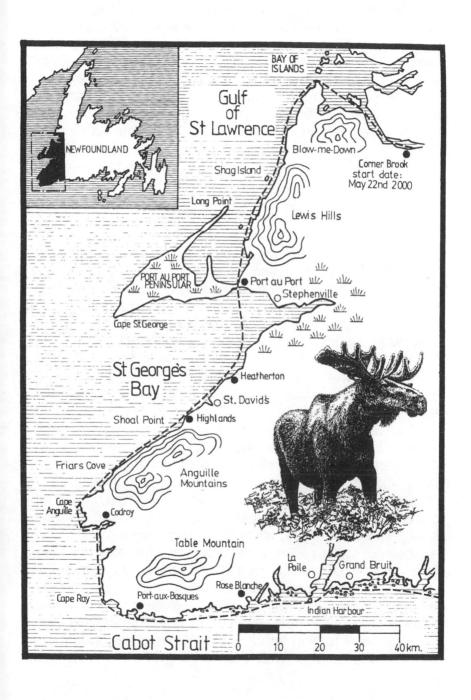

BAY OF ISLANDS

Gulf
of
St Lawrence

Blow-me-Down

Corner Brook
start date:
May 22nd 2000

NEWFOUNDLAND

Shag Island

Lewis Hills

Long Point

PORT AU PORT
PENINSULAR

Port au Port

Stephenville

Cape St George

St George's
Bay

Heatherton

St. David's

Shoal Point

Highlands

Friars Cove

Anguille
Mountains

Cape
Anguille

Codroy

Table Mountain

La
Poile

Grand Bruit

Rose Blanche

Cape Ray

Port-aux-Basques

Indian Harbour

Cabot Strait

0   10   20   30   40 km.

I left Bob and his friends standing at the Yacht Club Wharf in Corner Brook at 9:30 am. It was May 22/2000. The weather was clear and blue and a slight tailbreeze was coming from the mouth of the Humber River, heading down to the Bay of Islands and open sea twenty miles away. I struck a paddle rhythm early, had a blush on my face by noon, and by 4:00 pm, was starting to believe that summer had come early. The sun was glaring down, and with a light tailbreeze pushing me along, I couldn't have asked for a better start. In fact, I was beginning to think that I was overly dressed. Then just like a temperamental child that always seems to be teetering on the edge of a tantrum, the weather changed.

Bob had warned me that in May, the weather could go from a warm breeze to a polar blizzard in less than ten minutes. I'd taken what he'd said with a pinch of salt, but I was now a believer. God, did it ever blow! Of course, it helps if it starts blowing at the mouth of a bay, that you are passing a deep inlet which is guarded by a mountain aptly name Blow-Me-Down, and that dark clouds are obscuring the sun like the frayed ends of a nun's robe. It wasn't funny; but who wants to turn tail and give into your first Newfie breeze? Only two hours before, the bay smiled at me; now it was frothing at the mouth through sharpened teeth. It happened so quickly, it almost flipped over my kayak. I wasn't so much leaning into the wind, as free-falling towards the sea. For one interminable hour, I stuck my chin out, aligned my eyes on a point of land on the northern shore, and gunned it.

Bedazzled by danger one minute and becalmed by necessity the next. Ten strokes, that's all it took to go from confused seas of flying whitecaps, to glassly calm. I scooted behind some rocks, beached, lit a cigarette, cracked open a bottle of brandy, then started asking questions. On my sea chart, the bay's eastern shore had looked protected, but such is the fantasy of maps. If these off-shore winds were going to turn into a daily occurrence, then I could easily see myself turning into an alcoholic, and if I thought the warm glow of alcohol would improve my day, one quick look towards the open sea soon sobered me. Whitecaps were forming around the point ahead and squinting at me something evil. I could distinctly hear the muffled thuds of waves on rock, even though they were over a mile away. If ever I craved a baptism of fire, then this was the occasion.

Everything that day seemed larger than life; the steep snowcapped mountains that walled in the bay, the islands at its mouth that sprouted out vertically from the sea in huge knuckles of rock, the menacing clouds, angry seas, and the ferocious down draft of wind that I experienced crossing the inlet to Lark Harbour.

Rounding the point at the base of the Murray Mountains, at the lip of the Bay of Islands, was like falling into an abyss. Suddenly, it was very open, windy and very, very cold. I was still neither acclimatized to the conditions, or anywhere close to being a lean, mean paddling machine. My body was still coated in city flab and my well of endurance didn't even fill a bucket. To put it bluntly, I was exhausted. When you get weary this early in a trip, you tire quickly. The dimmer switch that tells you that you are passing from light to dark, is immediate. The last vestiges of energy left me with the first blast of cold air, rounding South Head. I was now riding large sea swells, rising and falling, craning this way and that, in search of any place to beach. I threw in the towel at Trumpet Cove. I spotted a pebbled beach no bigger than a postage stamp, under the shadow of South Head's lighthouse beacon; but then beggars can't be choosers.

From the look of the beach - with its distinctive, steep layers of pebbles and backdrop of twisted driftwood pushed up against a vertical face of rock - it had been formed by dangerous breakers. Luckily for me, the tide was fully in. Waves pushed up fiercely, then flattened out in false anger on the top of the beach, but any minute, the tide would start to fall. In thirty minutes these waves would start rising steeply into breakers, and I knew that I wouldn't have the strength to brace against them. Being sucked under by a strong riptide is one thing; having your kayak snapped in two on your first day is another.

Death or embarrassment? Neither option seemed worth the risk of waiting to find a better landing spot. It would be now or never. I caught a wave, surfed it gently, then grazed the shore not five feet from where I would make camp........ perfect.

You didn't have to be a rocket scientist to read the signs. There was only one patch of pebbles I could possibly camp on. Shaped like a kettle's lid on a three sided volcano with a backdrop of vertical rock, there would be no escape if the morning tide rose any higher than it was now, but at that moment, I was too tired and cold to care. I dragged my kayak onto a rocky ledge, tied it firmly to the twisted mass of driftwood that surrounded it, then erected my tent.

Some of the tent pegs took purchase, but most didn't. The tent took on a rather drunken look, but it was up and that's all that mattered. Luckily, I didn't have to cook. Mary had packed ample sandwiches to get me through the day, and then, there was the left-over pizza.

The sun lit up the night sky in a blaze of colour. The bay's islands burned in a magnificent collage of red, amber and purple. Large moving patterns twisted and banked like smudges in the dusk. A huge flock of ducks, chased by the approaching night sky, turned away on seeing me, then disappeared 'round the point. Before the first stars twinkled, the sea flattened. The wind had died completely, and I felt alone for the first time since the voyage had begun.

Later, I built a fire the size of a pyramid out of driftwood. It illuminated my small beach, danced around the cliff, and talked to me in words that crackled and spat. It centered the world of my first day, warmed my soul, and aided with cupfulls of tea mixed with brandy, cushioned my thoughts like a pillow.

I poked my nose out of the tent often that night to check on the tide's progress. The air was crisp, cold, and invigorating and the sky was blanketed in stars. The last time I checked, waves lapped at the foot of my tent, but were receding. In the deep silence, the vapour of my breath floated from my mouth to form clouds in the tent. I had to pinch myself. Was this a dream or reality? I had been too excited to sleep, but when I eventually rose into the early morning rays, I knew the trip had started.

I know now, how aging hockey players feel after the first day of training camp. My lower back had fused and when straightened, hurt; my legs wobbled like a drunken sailor's and my knees were sore; my hands refused to open on command, and my eyes stung from the combination of yesterday's wind, salt and sun. "Doesn't it feel beautiful to be alive?" I asked myself.

Whoever coined the nickname, "The Rock", for Newfoundland, deserves a medal; rock, rock and more rock. It's beautiful, impressive and intimidating, and if the conditions had not been in my favour that day, I doubt my nerves could have taken it so early in the trip.

As it was, I couldn't have asked for a better start to my second morning. It was clear and breathless, and I was in a rush to greet it. The sea was as flat as a mill-pond and crystal clear. Ahead and above, rocks and points of land leaped out like castle ramparts in defiance of the sea, and below, its shoreline protruded out into the water in aprons of rock. A lone seal - nose in the air breathing deeply - on spotting me, slapped its flipper, breaking the silence, then shot under my kayak like a cannon shell.

Within the same hour, three glistening backs appeared. They were dolphins; three puffs of vapour, three circles of motion, then plop! They were gone. For fifteen minutes they slowly arced out of the water, edging towards me, but as they neared my kayak, they changed course. Suddenly, in the blink of an eye, while two crashed out of the water in front, a third shot under my kayak like a spiralling bullet. Further on, half hidden by a shoal under the shadow of Fish Head, I disturbed a flock of ducks. They rose in a tremendous cloud of beating wings, splintered apart and regrouped as a squadron, then circled towards the sun. I was mesmerized, and for five minutes, stopped and followed their progress until they were lost out to sea.

I had expected to see lots of wild life, but what I didn't expect, was to see much evidence of fishing. Lobster traps buoys dotted the coastline like balloons floating on water, and by late afternoon the distant flash of speedboats glistening in the sun, was becoming a regular occurrence. Like bees searching for nectar, they would stop and start, zig and zag from one buoy to the next, searching for lobsters. The season must have opened, and when two fishermen dropped by for a late afternoon chat near Shag Island, I was more than receptive.

It goes without saying, that fishing is not just a tradition in Newfoundland, it's in their DNA, and being in a boat myself, I could expect the occasional question either about its performance or the sanity of its owner.

I love these questions and never get bored of them. I look upon my kayak much like a woman looks upon a garter belt. It's a bait, a tease, something to grab your attention, and over the years, it has opened many more doors than it has closed. Traveling is my stage. It's the only time that I can feel my balls. If you met me in a bar or on the street, I'm no different than your average Joe, but put me in a kayak and I sprout wings and fly. All those inhibitions that I suffer from - my frightful shyness, my terrible panic attacks, and my paralyzing lack of confidence - they all float away in a sea breeze, and my usual lock-jaw turns into a case of raging gabbla-dictums.

"That's a little boat ya got there me boy. Where's ya going?"

"'Round the Rock, mate," I replied. His jaw dropped into his chest, but his buddy, rose to the occasion.

"Aye ya got more guts than sense. I've got a spare motor if tha wants...........On medication are we?"

On hearing that, we all burst out laughing. Ice broken, a lively discussion ensued. Male bonding par excellence, but at that moment, wine, women and song weren't high on the agenda. My most pressing need at that moment, was for local knowledge of the shoreline ahead. Sea charts aren't really worth the paper they are printed on and the same goes for the Maritime Weather Forecasts. They are all geared towards off-shore vessels. Bays, capes and points of land generate their own conditions, and that is why I put so much importance on local knowledge.

I would be paddling over the same waters these men would fish. Our meeting was like the answer to a maiden's prayer, so when they had exhausted their whys and wherefors, I jumped in.

"What's it like down the coast?" I was immediately taken through the A to Z of sunkers, clapping waves, riptides, off-shore winds, bad shoal water, then, what I dreaded the most........ FOG!

"Watch out crossing St. George's Bay. Your boat's just a speed bump to fishermen," and then said, more as an after thought than to frighten me, "If one of those big buggers hits ya, ya'll be a gonna. There was a near miss in fog two summers ago. A couple kayakers from Stephenville capsized in a longliner's wake. T'other was brushed. Could easily have drowned. These waters are chilly, me boy," and to emphasize this point, he opened his overalls to show me his dry suit. "Remember, you're not even a blip on their radar screens."

I must have looked like a scolded child, because no sooner had his words sunk in, when he changed the subject.

"Can you roll this thing?"

"No," I said with a laugh. "If the weather's bad, I stay on land."

I had obviously told him what he had wanted to hear because my reply spawned another galaxy of questions, and by the time they, too, had run their course, we had spent the better part of an hour shooting the breeze. Then on parting, with the same ease that old friends offer their hands to be shaken, I was offered an evening invitation.

"Does you want a cooked supper?"

When I was younger, I would have given my eye teeth for a good night of sex, but now I am older and wiser, and even more to the point, my stomach was already churning.

"Yes!" I nearly bit his hands off. "Where's your camp?"

I followed a stubby finger, attached to a hand the size of a sledge hammer, to a chisel sized crack in the hills. There, stuck like a limpet on a fold of rock, surrounded by dark pebbles with a view of an opal sea that most city folk would give their back teeth to spend a weekend in, was their home away from home; four plain square walls and a roof...... paradise!

If yesterday was hot, then today felt like being in a pressure cooker. I was on the water before sunrise. It was frigid. I could see my own breath, but by mid morning everything was bleached. Long Point, a ten mile sand bar that tips the Port-au-Port Peninsula, was starting to float, shimmer, then lose itself to a heat haze. The coastal cliffs had a glazed look about them and the sea was smoking.

I had already made up my mind before starting in Corner Brook, that I'd not paddle around this exposed peninsula. Working out in a gym and fine tuning your body while paddling are one kind of challenge, testing your nerves against a twenty mile crossing of open sea between Cape St. George to St. David's across St. George's Bay so early in the trip is another. I didn't feel as if I had anything to prove. I'd crossed large bodies of water before, but the seduction of portaging a causeway of gravel, topped by a road that connects the Port- au-Port Peninsula to the mainland, and thereby halving the distance across the bay, was too good to pass up.

The sea was as smooth as a freshly groomed skating rink and just as enticing; huge tables of rock sailed beneath my kayak, then a slight breeze, a hint of ripple, and the picture would wash away. Again, lobster fishermen came calling. My name was being passed down the coast and I was slowly becoming public property. News travels like a wildfire in remote regions. These unplanned trips of mine seem to take on lives of their own and this one was proving to be no different.

Past Buff Head, the coastal cliffs dropped away and Newfoundland's interior of rolling hills and wooded forest were laid bare. A distant blue haze announced the Long Range Mountains and the dusty brown of its foothills of fern and moss.

I took a pit-stop just before Fox Island River, having been enticed by the sight of a perfectly groomed beach. It had everything; a tidal lagoon to swim in, ample driftwood for a fire and clean, running water to drink. I should have stopped early, stayed, made camp and taken an early night. I was already beginning to feel the effects of sunburn. The skin on my face felt as if stretched on a rack, and already, blisters were forming on the palms of my hands. The pinched nerve between my shoulder blades hurt like hell and my knees, still sore from the first day, were starting to turn blue. After all, I wasn't in a hurry, but my adrenalin was pumping.....

Big mistake to continue, for no sooner had I entered the mouth of the bay and started my long haul to its throat, when the Roaring Forties struck. Thank God the Port-au-Port Bay is shallow and sheltered from ocean currents. The wind was so strong that it shaved off the tops of waves, picked up surf like spit and struck my eyes like needles. It was soul destroying, like a toothache that wont go away. After an hour, salt had formed on my face, like a second skin, and my knuckles had gone from purple to white. It took me almost two hours of constant paddling to cover five miles.

I made the causeway by midafternoon, beaten to a snot, too tired to go any further, and kicking myself for not stopping earlier. The gravel causeway looked like the Great Wall of China, and at that moment, just as insurmountable; but mood swings, like coastal weather, don't last long.

"How's it going, me boy?" The voice came from above and for a split second haloed behind the sun, God sent, but sunstroke and fatigue can do that to you. " Me name's Art Hynes. Ah knows yours. Ya Bernie, the kayaker, aren't ya?"

Unbeknown to me, I'd been under his watchful eye for

the last two hours. He lived in a trailer within a stone's throw from where I'd beached. Through his binoculars, my appearance down the bay had been like the second coming, and for me his appearance was a stroke of luck. Art had spotted my little yellow kayak almost before I'd seen the causeway. He'd not only seen me struggling down the bay, but days before, had listened to the interview I'd given CBC in Corner Brook. He had remembered that I'd said, "I may take the inside route and portage over the causeway." He'd been glued to the window all day; half hoping, half expecting for me to come. Now that I had dropped into his lap, he wasn't going to take no for an answer.

"Leave your stuff there, Bernie. Nobody 'al bother it. Come up ta house. I got a brew on."

Not only did he offer me a shower, a magnificent lobster supper washed down with wine, the keys to his video collection and a night between clean sheets, but he also trucked my kayak over the causeway and down to a secluded beach on the shore of St. George's Bay before nightfall.

Next morning, while Art flipped eggs and fried some bacon, I used his phone to call the weather bureau's taped hourly forecast:

23.05.2000
wind east 10 to 15 km/hr.
light becoming east 30 km/hr after midnight
24.05.2000
east 20km/hr
afternoon fog and rain beginning

Perfect conditions for the day, and after putting down the phone, I proceeded to spade down Art's breakfast, pack away his Tim Horton's donuts, fill my flask full of his coffee, then accept his lift to the beach.

It was a gorgeous crossing; light breezes all the way and no swell. I was a little nervous at the beginning, but it's always like that the first time you let go of land, and I was glad to get it under my belt. I was always weary of the wind, keeping one eye on the shore and taking in cloud formations with the other. Sometimes, I think that I burn more energy on nervous exhaustion than on actual paddling. To be truthful, I didn't really relax into the crossing until I was almost within spitting distance of the other side of the bay. It had taken me four hours to cover twelve miles. Not fast, but then it wasn't a race.

Just past Heatherton, a strong northeasterly picked up. Immediately, the temperature plummeted; the coastline ahead turned a milky grey, and within minutes, the sea was boiling. I was skirting close to shore, being pushed on at a jogger's pace and eating up the mileage. Suddenly, I got cramps. Those earlier nervous twitches had locked into one continuous jolt of pain. At first, it was concentrated in my lower thigh, but soon spread like a cancer to my groin. The pain put a damper on my progress.... enough was enough.

Take-offs and landings have never been one of my strong points. I am an endurance man. I don't possess the upper body strength that one expects a kayaker to have, and am more of a finesse paddler. I usually use my hips to balance, not paddle blades, go over waves, not through them, and as for surfing.... forget it. So why I chose this particular beach to come ashore, when I must have passed half a dozen places that were sheltered by sand bars, God only knows. It's not that the waves were big, but they were cresting. It's not that I didn't have time to think, I had. Timing a wave is essential because if you hit it too early, it will pass underneath your kayak, and if you hit it too late, it will crest on your head.

I actually judged the wave perfectly, but didn't see an approaching cross-wave. I had been textbook perfect up until the point of no return. I had waited just outside the breaker zone for a lull, then paddled hard. The wave picked me up like a feather. I started to surf. I was actually enjoying the moment, then the cross-wave hit. It knocked me sideways, filled up the trough of the wave I'd been surfing and pushed me back.

Now, when the backwash is stronger than your forward momentum, you stop, get sucked back, then freeze for the inevitable onrush of surf from behind..... are you still with me?

I saw the wave cresting over my shoulder. It looked huge, but then anything from ground zero looks huge. There I was, trapped in gortex, knees jammed, arms flailing, bracing this way and that, and skidding ever so slowly sideways. I was now being pushed along by a wall of surf. It swallowed my paddle, then my shoulder, then I kissed the sand.... chit! I hate coming ashore in breakers.

If you have ever pissed in your pants, you know how it is to feel water running down your legs. Even wearing a skin tight wet suit, I was soaked from head to foot, and with a cold northeasterly whipping around my ears, I was soon shaking with cold.

I fervently believe that if I fell face down into pig chit, I would come up smelling of roses, for no sooner had I dragged my kayak above the high tide mark and started to unload my gear, when yet another invitation materialized in front of me.

"Eh boy, that's a fine rig ya got."

To him, I must have looked like a cat on a hot tin roof. I was hopping around, trying to force blood into my joints, and my teeth chattered uncontrollably.

"Bring your stuff up to me cabin. I'll get ya a cuppa."

Sixty minutes later, I found myself bathed in heat. I had been offered a night in a weekend-cabin built for fun. My clothes were pegged-out around its stove in colourful streamers, pickled rabbit was warming in a pan, and I was stretched out on a couch, watching the rain come down. My newfound friend only stayed the time it took for me to change, then left for Stephenville. Payment would be by postcard, a note of thanks from the finish line. Now, that's hospitality......

I woke next morning before dawn to the sight of white-caps marching out of the bay in well-ordered rows. It was cozy in the cabin, and I didn't relish the thought of taking them on so early in the morning, so I rolled over and went back to sleep.

The next I remembered, it was noon. If anything, the wind had picked up, but the sky was clear. I had been told there were plenty of places ahead to beach, so I was neither worried about the lateness of the day nor about the conditions.

Leaving the bay, the whole coastline was dotted with fish camps. They came into sight like charcoal drawings, some abandoned, and some inhabited with speedboats resting on angled ramps. Occasionally, spotted by children on shore, shouts and windmills of greeting would come my way, dogs would bark, and on more than one occasion, lobster fishermen dropped what they were doing with their traps and swung by in their speedboats for a chat.

Today's plan was to paddle only to the small summer fishing community called Highlands. I had been forewarned that the section from Shoal Point to Cape Anguille, some twenty-two miles, was the longest and most dangerous stretch of unbroken shoreline in Newfoundland. I'd heard that it was all cliff with few escape routes, and at this time of year, prone to bad weather. I wanted to get as close to these cliffs as possible, hope and pray for good weather, then gun-it.

By midafternoon, the weather had closed down completely. Dark clouds obliterated the sun, rain flew horizontally and the wind cut to the bone. Ahead points of land lay out like rows of spilled carrots. I could just make out Shoal Point through the rain, and beyond to the fainter but higher cliffs that drop down vertically from the Anguille Mountain Range to the sea.

I turned into shore at Highlands and almost immediately fell under the spell of a man named Russell Noseworthy. I was actually sitting down and having tea and biscuits with a group of guys I had spoken to earlier in the day, when Russell walked into their cabin and into my life.

"Who we got here? Are you the one kayaking around Newfoundland? Up for a drink me boy?"

I never stood a chance. There I was; my brain wrapped around tomorrow's paddle, craving an early night, wishing now that I had chosen some uninhabited place down the coast to put up my tent. My body craved food, not drink, and my brain, some quiet spot to prepare itself mentally for the challenges ahead, but Russell had other ideas for the evening.

"Let's go to the Legion."

How could I refuse? Russell was a giant in all directions. His size alone, if not his forceful personality, wouldn't take no for an answer. He was one of those people who's sure of his own good fortune, not shy to tell you that he always caught the first lobster of the season, had the most traps planted, and was the first person on the water every morning. As if to emphasize his gifts of his recovery...."Don't worry, I'll have you back before dawn." He had a silver tongue, an infectious laugh that spread like a plague, and as I would find out later in the Legion, a gift with women. He promised I'd get laid, at the very least drunk, and luckily that night, I got neither.

The Legion turned out better than I had expected. I was a star. Almost everyone there had heard about my trip and were dying to hear my stories. Faces around our table soon swelled with drink and excitement. The volume curved up into the night, and eyes that only hours before had squinted in the smoke, now opened like saucers, blood-shot and glazed. Conversations stretched from the sedate debate of university coffee houses to the colour of women's knickers, but that was only our first venue. We ended the night sitting around a kitchen table of Russell's uncle's, eating moose and drinking shorts. Maybe it was the alcohol that loosened my tongue, or just plain curiosity, but when Russell started to talk about jacking it all in, of leaving Codroy in search of more permanent employment, I couldn't help asking about the state of the fisheries.

"What's the guideline for allocating lobster licenses?"

You'd think I'd just dropped in from Mars. The room went silent, then Russell spoke up.

"Fuckin' terrible problem."

I should never have broached the subject. I'd let the genie out of the bottle, and try as I may, I couldn't stuff it back in.

"We're just like migrant farm workers. All we do is harvest. They don't even give us licenses where we live. I'm one of the lucky ones. I'm from Codroy. It's less than an hour's drive away from here. I could drive here and back every day if I want, but most people you see in Highlands aren't that lucky. My mate, Jim is from Lark Harbour, David is from Port-aux-Basques. Try and make sense of that. It cost money to build those cabins you see in Highlands, and that's all they are. You've seen them. Some are just made of plywood, four square walls and a roof. If you're not working on one of those bloody factory boats, you need a chest full of licenses just to exist. We moves from one species to another, catches what they tell us, takes what they pay us. We got no control over any of the fisheries now. We don't make the decisions, just does what we're told. We live by rules made somewhere else by some son-a-bitches don't know nothing about this place. Puts that in your book, me boy."

I know, I should have never told Russell that I was going to write a book about my trip, but I thought that I might as well get it over with. I like to scratch under the surface of places that I visit, get my hands dirty, and find out what makes people tick. As my trip was solely a coastal one, it only stood to reason that fishermen would be my greatest source of information. I'd given him and his friends a platform to vent their feelings, so now I just sat back and listened. I had already been broadsided by an old man at the Legion. That man had witnessed fishing go from seasonal, inshore, small boats to deep water year-round factory ships and draggers. Some, as he said, were the size of small towns with their own recreational rooms, bars and video cinemas.

"The fish is all gone," he said, and the forest, as I had found out earlier in the week with Bob, was just about all cut down. "Ruined, polluted and wrecked," as Bob called it.

"No wonder there's ghosts here," I said. I had already passed many a skeleton fish camp with walls that were beginning to sag and cave in.

"Times are different," Russell continued, "It's chasing money and buying plastic speedboats and seamobiles. Now everyone is on first name terms with their bank managers, in debt to their eye balls, with more plastic in their wallets than you can shake a stick at." Then his uncle jumped in.

"You could say that before our flag was gutted and it sold its soul to the mainland, we were a proud lot. I'm not saying everything has changed for the worse, but welfare and quota systems are a cancer. You could say people was only kind in those days out of necessity. You couldn't afford enemies. In those days, it was one for all and all for one. You sank or swam together as a community. Sure, we don't have those diseases we had back then, no one is starving, we have schools, central heating, food banks, electricity, television, roads, cars, but you don't get owt for nowt in this life. Now there's drugs and crime, vandalism, everything's padlocked, and it's all in the name of welfare. You'll not find many Newfoundlanders who could say that they haven't a relative who doesn't work for the government. It's like the loonies running the insane asylum. Some of young uns will tell you that Newfoundland may have its roots on the rock, but has its branches on the mainland. When they tell you that, what they mean is that the cream has left for the mainland. There's no future in the fisheries, and everything else is just a glorified make-work-program."

It was a sad end to a glorious night, but I knew there was more than a grain of truth in his words. I had seen it in the boarded up windows of people's houses and the business "FOR SALE" signs in Corner Brook. I'd seen it in the sunken eyes of the youthful unemployed and in their listless walk. He'd just underlined the honest truth as he saw it, and I thanked him for his frankness.

True to his word, Russell had me back and bedded down before dawn, and when I woke up at sunrise, I was bursting with energy.

Chapter: 2
Life is Delicious

No matter how much you train physically indoors, nothing can prepare you mentally for the challenges ahead, and that day, I just felt lucky to be alive

I love to push the envelope, live on the edge, so to speak, but today I almost lost it. I don't have a death wish, but there is a fine line between courage and foolishness, and today I crossed it. The day started at 5:30 am with a fisherman's breakfast of cereal, followed by bacon and eggs. By 6:30 am, I was on the water. I had left under threatening clouds, a calculated risk. In front was the longest stretch of unbroken cliffs in Newfoundland, a twenty mile plus wall of rock with few escape routes. The Marine Weather Forecast had called for heavy rains, and winds from 40 - 60 km/hr. The winds were forecasted to be from the southeast; a tailwind, and had the winds been on-shore or headwinds, I would never have risked it.

All went well until Shoal Point. From here, the mountains rose directly out of the sea, as if cut with a butter knife. Today my nerves would be put under the microscope. Once I'd started there'd be no turning back, and with that thought in mind, I turned my kayak out to sea and into the tailwind.

One hour later, I was approaching Lewis Point. I was tucked in behind its face of rock. I had opened my thermos, was taking a coffee and cigarette break, when the rain started. Soon the cliff's vivid colours of amber and purple were lost to a torrential downpour. The sea started to bubble and hiss. I was soaked immediately. For the next twelve miles, the rain was relentless. Clifftop waterfalls sprang to life from nowhere. Hidden streams had turned into instant rivers and now emptied themselves into the sea in an awesome show of power.

By noon, the winds were blowing so strong that I spent more time bracing and correcting my steering than paddling. The waves weren't big, but steep, and every few minutes they would swamp me from behind. I was already sitting in a pool of sea water and the wind-driven rain was starting to trickle down my neck. My palms had turned into the colour of wax, and my fingers - even protected by wind deflecting poggies - had gone from the look of prunes to that of wrinkled raisins. While the day was not even half over, I was beginning to feel hypothermic. I had already eaten three of the six Mars Bars that were stored in my cockpit for emergency, and my thermos of hot coffee was three quarters empty.

The cliffs seemed to stretch on forever. Even the impressive rock formations in front of Friar's Cove with their distinctive buttress of rock, rising out of the sea like a gothic cathedral of splintered spires and steeples, seemed if anything, to recede with time into the distance. At one point, I was startled by a loud crack from above. A rock had loosened itself and brought its neighbours down into the water like a cluster of motor shells. I wasn't in any immediate danger, but still, it was a close call. I was paddling as near to the foot of the cliffs as was feasible, seeking shelter from the wind. My back, forever cold and chilled from the constant wind, was now racked in pain that no matter how I moved around in my cockpit, would not go away.

Friars Cove offered me only a respite, for no sooner had I entered it, when I saw it was occupied. On spotting me, thousands of none-to-pleased ducks started to flex their muscles and complain. The noise was deafening. I should have stayed longer, but working on the principle of last in, first to leave, I left after a short break.

I encountered the first signs of life at Cape John and met two lobster fishermen. I didn't know who was crazier, them or me. Their boat, heading into the wind, seemed to spend more time out of the water than in. It would rear up out of the water like a wild stallion, then crash back down with a sickening thud.

By now, my wrists felt like grated sandpaper, and finding any semblance of a paddle rhythm was hopeless, but meeting the fishermen had raised my spirits. They'd told me that if I cut straight across from Snakes Blight to Cape Anguille, I'd bi-pass the Cape's tidal rip close to shore and miss most of the Blight's strong off-shore winds; but the best of their offering came when they told me that if I kept up a steady pace, I should make Codroy by supper time.

I was cold, wet and tired, but the thought of turning down Snakes Blight, putting up my tent in the rain, not knowing what tomorrow's weather would hold, and certainty that I would have to begin the day in a cold, damp wet suit, was too much to contemplate. At that moment, all I could think of was Russell's invitation to sleep in his empty house in Codroy; have a shower, dry my clothes and sleep in comfort. I now shut down the wind and rain, and held onto his invitation as if my life depended on it.

Rounding Cape Anguille was a nightmare. The current and wind were in conflict and at the Cape's apex, the seas were angry and confused. I was more than a little frightened, not of the seas, but of my fatigue. Once again, I shut down my surroundings and anchored my eyes on a rock in some sheltered waters. I was on automatic pilot. I had already paddled over thirty miles; no great distance if you're fighting fit, but my second wind had come and gone. It was now a paddle of survival, a head game. The only thing that now kept me going, was the thought of Russell's house.

It took me over an hour to round Cape Anguille. It was 4:00 pm when I spotted its lighthouse and the first signs of life on land in ten hours, but still I wasn't home. Not for the first time on my travels, life played a cruel joke. The entrance to Codroy's harbour wasn't where it should have been according to my sea chart, and in my fatigue, I got lost. Codroy Island - as I found out later - had been recently connected to the mainland by a wall of rock. Before that, the northern entrance to the harbour had been an open channel; now it was a breakwater of rock, and when I realized that I would have to kayak around the island and add another one and half miles through a strong headwind to my day, I started to cry.

After eleven hours in the saddle, I finally made Codroy. I had paddled over thirty five miles, fought hypothermia and pushed my body to its very threshold. Thank God, a welcoming committee of curious onlookers awaited my arrival. I was so tired that I didn't so much peel my body out of my kayak's cockpit, as fall out of it, hardly able to stand. What a pathetic sight I must have made. Now I know what it feels like to be given a second chance. I sat there on the wharf like a wet puppy-dog, hearing voices, but unable to speak. At one point, I put my head between my knees and wept quietly. I don't think I have ever been that tired. My stomach was knotted, my throat parched and my muscles were on fire. I was telling myself "never again", but knew it was a lie.

Forty-five minutes later, kayak stored in the fish plant, wearing Craigh Collior's track suit while mine rattled in his dryer, I found myself unwinding into a fresh crab sandwich. He'd taken me under his wing and later, his wife prepared a fried cod supper with all the trimmings. That night, I ate like there was no tomorrow, drank gallons of tea, then staggered back up the hill to Russell's house.

I woke into back spasms, and the only muscle used that morning, was to operate the TV remote. Today, my body was going to go knowhere. I ate and slept, slept and ate, and visitors came and went. Although I did try to be receptive, play my part, I could neither muster the energy nor the enthusiasm to enjoy their company. My tanks were empty, but by nightfall, a fall colour had returned to my cheeks.

Craig woke me the next morning at 4:30 am with a breakfast invitation. Outside, it was damp and cold, but what's new, you may ask. Some days Newfoundland can take your breath away, and that morning was one of those occasions. The coastline ahead, with its shades of grey, tinges of purple and oily black sea, that on any other day under wind, would have almost certainly sent me back to sleep, now looked spellbinding.

I headed out into a light headwind, but once past Larkin

Point, the wind not only picked-up, but it started to rain; rain... rain... bloody rain.

I was beginning to believe that Newfoundland could make a fortune if only it could harvest its rain for international export. Maybe they could strike up some reciprocal deal with the Saudi Royal Family and exchange sun for clouds and rock for sand. Who knows, on reading this, maybe some youthful entrepreneur could patent the idea. If Newfoundland can sell ice from icebergs to the Japanese, then anything is possible.

Daydreaming wasn't the only thing to enter my mind that morning. The constant and ever increasing headwinds were wearing me down. I carry two paddles for this reason - wide blades for power, narrow blades for low resistance in headwinds - but it seems that whatever advantage could be gained by changing during the day, was always outweighed by the thought of having to break my rhythm, stop and get blown back, just for the sake of changing paddle width. I always have the same argument in my head, at the beginning of all my trips, and today's decision was no different than the others. I chose my wide blade paddle and for the rest of the trip, never changed, no matter which way the wind blew......... bloody minded, yes, but why tinker with something that has worked before?

Progress was good until I entered the narrow channel between Cape Ray's lighthouse and its off-shore reef. Its riptide was against me. I proceded at a snail's pace, forever searching for back eddies close to shore and keeping well away from whirlpools, but no sooner had I put it all behind and started a slow arc of the shallow cape, when I was exposed to large sea swells. I was gob smacked! In front were the biggest waves I'd seen to date.

The seas around the cape are influenced by two currents. It's here were the strong currents of the Cabot Strait collide with that of the Gulf of St. Lawrence. At that moment, it wasn't so much this fact or the large sea swells that bothered me, but the shoal waters ahead. They extended out further than I could see. I had no idea how many cresting waves or surf I would have to puncture before reaching the relative safety of deep water. Half submerged boulders spread out in front like spilled marbles and the surf gave its seas the look of a chess board. Was the tide coming in or going out?

What an exhilarating ride! It was ten times easier than it looked because the surf had little punch and it was easy to spot where the sunkers were. In deep water, the waves although huge, were rounded and easy to paddle in. If any-thing, I felt a little sea sick, and it was with this nauseating feeling in the pit of my stomach, and the thought that at any moment, my breakfast might decorate my boat, that I turned towards the shoreline as soon as I could.

I had not been ashore five minutes, when Newfoundland's hospitality swallowed me up again. A passer-by stopped his truck, helped me pull my kayak ashore, then gave me a lift to the nearest house. In the past, I have said that just turning up unannounced on someone's doorstep during a trip and offering myself up as a story, turned me into an instant extended family member, more than willing to be passed down from father to son, from aunt to niece, and that it was payment enough for a night between clean sheets. But this everyday hospitality was becoming downright embarrassing.

Example: I met Russell Graham on the internet. I had constructed a website so that people could follow my trip. Russell had found my site, hotmailed me and insisted that I come to Port-aux-Basques for a visit. I was now taking him up on his offer. I telephoned him from Jerret Point and one hour later, I was relaxing in an easy chair; a glass of brandy in one hand and the other wrapped around a cheese and ham sandwich. Life is delicious........yeh, boy.

That night, I was wined and dined. It never ceases to amaze me that human nature, given half the chance, can be so warm and open to strangers. Maybe it was my form of transportation, maybe it was my Irish charm and fun lov-ing ways, or maybe the old saying, "God looks after his cho-sen fools" has more than just a grain of truth in its message.

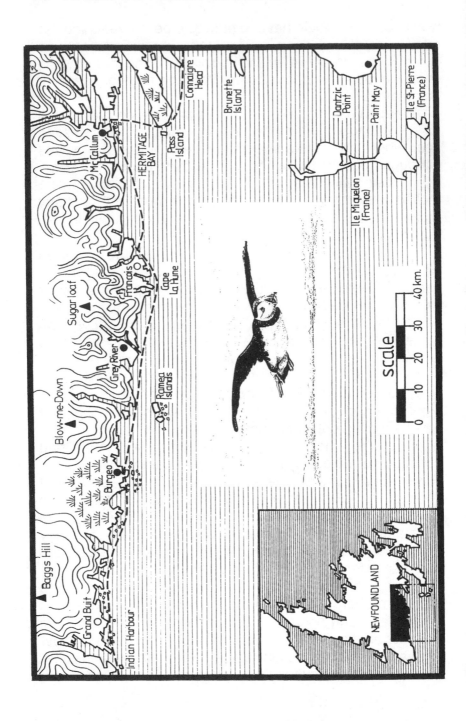

Chapter: 3
The Southern Shore

From Port-aux-Basques, you enter what is commonly called the Southern Shore. That day, I was hoping to make it to the end of the road to Rose Blanche. From there, I'd be on my own. From Rose Blanche to McCallum, I would be paddling past at least half a dozen year-round isolated communities. This stretch of over 100 miles of coastline - as a crow flies - is devoid of road traffic as the only way in and out is by boat or plane. It's these isolated areas that fuel my trips. It's the reason that I take risks. I had already paddled down the Gulf of St. Lawrence and visited many of its isolated communities on the Quebec Lower North Shore. I had also battled through snow and ice and Atlantic storms to visit the even more isolated communities on the Labrador coast. Now, I couldn't wait to experience the same sense of isolation on Newfoundland's Southern Shore.

I have always been seduced by these far away places; the ones cut off from road, with rhythms governed more by natural forces than the flick of a switch, that are more inward than outward looking, and where neighbours rely more on each other than government for help. On the surface you'd think that you had just stepped back in time, but that's just an illusion. Even on the most isolated beaches, you will find the modern-day flotsam of life washed up on its shorelines. Already, I'd seen plastic containers, a television, shards of broken glass, numerous empty boxes and always, torn nets. The sea not only swallows up garbage, but also shuffles it around like a pack of cards. It's not so much the trappings of life that are different about these communities, but it's their way of life, which to me is as precious and endangered as the rarest species on earth. Too lose a unique way of life is to lose a colour from its tapestry. For me, the people who inhabit these communities are vivid red. These people have passion, character and a sense of place that is completely lost in today's urban life. I've seen and experienced it all before, but never tire of it.

These places are full of tradition and I love them. I love those mint green homes with borders of red sash around their windows and unique add-ons, the ones that branch out from shed to mansion, with their natural bends and tilts. I enjoy seeing rows of work boots that seem to stand guard at every doorway. The smell of wood fires, oven fresh bread and clothes lines fluttering like multi-coloured prayer flags in a breeze all put a smile in my heart. Who cares if their gardens are the size of postage stamps, that you see potato flowers, not rose petals, and cabbage leaves, not herbs? Who cares if you have to pick through a minefield of junk and the occasionally rabid dog to get to a doorstep? I love those trails of gravel, not asphalt and boardwalks that are not paved. If life there was easy, anesthetic and tame, these places wouldn't be different, and Bernie would not be paddling towards one, especially on a day like today.

It was as windy as Hell and there was a headwind to boot. Sunkers were everywhere and the sea looked as if someone had pulled a dark bedsheet over a lively snakepit. There were confused seas; clapping waves and surf bubbles flew through the air like soap married to water.

Why was I on the sea? Good question. That morning, the writing was on the wall, but I'd listened to the weather forecast; damn the CBC radio, damn the Sea Gods, and damn myself for being so cocky. It wasn't all gloom and doom. Even under such hellish conditions, the coastline, windswept and in places treeless, looked magnificent.

Near Isle-aux-Morts, I landed through some exhilarating four foot surf that I'd actually paddled into just for the hell of it. I was finding my sea legs and if anything, was beginning to enjoy the conditions. Near Rose Blanche the wind died, then within minutes, did a U turn so that I was now paddling with the wind in my sails. I was on cloud nine, and when I eventually paddled through a narrow channel, under the watchful gaze of one of Canada's oldest stone built lighthouses (now a bed and breakfast) into the picture-perfect harbour of Rose Blanche, it made my day.

Most people, who have never visited Newfoundland, carry some romantic picture of a quaint harbour in their heads; one that is guarded by angry rocks at its mouth with a horseshoe harbour surrounded by colourful, wooden square houses with stepped-down fishing stages built on stilts over the sea. The image that I have, is of Rose Blanche. Trust the French influence to find romance on a desolate stretch of coast. One minute, I was paddling in rogue waves and the next, gliding over a mirrored surface with an amphitheatre backdrop of houses that appeared as though carved out of rock. The only thing that I could think of, as I paddled between barnacled and weeded fishing stage pilons, was that I had to sleep on one..... this one!

I kayaked up to the first pair of feet I saw, explained myself - what I was doing and where I wanted to pitch my tent - then leaned into his reply like a spoiled child.

"Ne' problem me boy. Ya can sleep in my shed. I'll fire up stove for ya."

That night, sleeping on top of my sleeping bag, half naked, massaged in heat, belly full of cod fried in salt pork, pushed into sleep by the ripples of a rising tide, and surrounded by the sounds, smells and sight of a fisherman's trade, I fell blissfully asleep.

The next morning, I was on the water by 6:00 am. My stomach was bursting with a good old Scotsman's breakfast of sticky porridge, cooked in salted water, with cream and melted butter for a topping. I couldn't ask for a better send-off, but once again the gods were teasing me.

I started paddling in seas still influenced by yesterday's strong winds. A sea was on, but the wind was still sleeping. Storm clouds were queuing up over the horizon, but looked hours away. Ahead, the coastline looked like the chipped edges of a broken plate, dotted with small islands and interspersed with mushrooms of rock. The sun beat down during those first few hours and burned my skin. I used my sun glasses and a baseball cap to shade my eyes for the first time on my trip. I was finding it difficult to use my sea chart; islands fused together in the sun's glare and points of land wobbled, separated, floated, then seemed to melt back into the sea. At the Big Seal, I decided to cut diagonally across open water to West Point, but almost immediately, the sun disappeared. I'd just let go of land, started my ten mile paddle of open sea, when the threatening northeasterly struck.

I wasn't worried at first, but as the shoreline slipped away and I paddled further out to the sea, the wind got stronger. I was now three miles out, paddling in the pushed up remnants of yesterday's heavy swell. It was like rising and falling in an elevator. I would lose sight of the land one minute, and the next, be given a roof top view. At least half a dozen times, I got soaked and probably changed course the same number. Once again, I misjudged my angles, lost sight of West Point in the heavy swell, and had it not been for a longliner, would still be out there searching for it. It appeared out of nowhere, like a ball of fire, a red glow on the horizon, then I lost it behind a hill. I stopped, took a mental photograph, then paddled like crazy towards its memory.

Indian Harbour, wasn't even mentioned on my sea chart. Nestled inbetween two folds of hills with a narrow channel, it's one of those places that was too small for resettlement, yet too large to forget. I paddled into its sleepy, summer community of two families and immediately got a hero's welcome.

Apparently, it had never been an all-year-round community, but even so, the era of resettlement had killed it. Most of the houses, and there weren't many, were built by people from La Poile and Grand Bruit. They'd been built by men who had to live close to the fishing grounds, and the larger add-on houses by those who wanted to a have a family life; and what a life, when the inshore fisheries was fueled by man powered dorys .

Imagine no fences to keep out the ball, no cars to watch out for and no reason to lock your door at night. The people who greeted me that day, didn't have much. The cod moratorium hadn't reached this far south, but quotas were down and there was no work in the fishplant in La Poile. They shared with me what they had; tea, biscuits and cheese-spread sandwiches, but most of all, they shared themselves. I could have stayed longer, but I wanted to camp under the stars that night. As gracious as my hosts were, Newfoundland's hospitality was begining stifle my drive to continue the adventure, and the welcomed, but constant diet of homemade dinners was starting to bloat my stomach. I swear, I must have already gained five pounds of weight and had almost forgotten that I had a tent or even a stove. I stayed rooted to the kitchen table until the last sandwich had been eaten, then left with a promised post-card from the finish line

Crossing La Poile Bay, the view offered up was amazing. I could see all the way back to the snowcapped Long Range Mountains, their low-lying brown and grey hills and dusting of green. On the bay's traverse, a pod of minke whales crossed my path, then it was the turn of a flock of ducks. They opened up to allow me through, as if by magic. It took me less than an hour to cross the three mile bay, and lucky for me, the wind held its breath. At Eastern Point, I decided to take the sheltered inside passage behind Jacques Island and almost immediately, applauded my decision.

If Rose Blanche had offered up a picture-perfect harbour, then the place I found to camp on, with its perfect horseshoe beach of golden sand, was another form of heaven. Although it was only 4:00 pm and there was still plenty of daylight, there was no contest about where to stay. I beached, stripped naked and let the sun's rays kiss my flesh. It was a secluded playground par excellence; one that was sheltered, bathed in heat, surrounded by lush wood, spring-fed with plenty of spongy moss to camp on and filled with the sights and sounds of golden eagles. What a relaxing way to end a day. I built a fire of driftwood, cooked, ate and for once, turned in early.

I woke to the chirping of golden eagles. Every few minutes, I heard the rush of their feathers and followed their moving shadows as they zig-zagged across the beach. My every movement was being watched. Were they waiting for me to leave, or were they just curious? As I loaded my kayak, an eagle landed in a tree no more than twenty feet away. I could hear its talons grasping a branch, see its chest feathers tremble, the pupils of its eyes move, and the sharp hook of its beak. Was it winking at me?

A kayak is very quiet, but after awhile, the noise of water dripping from the paddles can seem deafening. It's times like these that I give into my imagination and allow it free range to travel. Sometimes, like today, I daydream of love; not the hot, sweaty times fueled by hormones, but the type that poets write about. Those timeless unions like your first love and want let go; the ones that, no matter how fast or far you run, cannot be escaped. These times are never good. They are a death knell to the solo voyageur. Lost loves; especially the ones sacrificed to travel, shoot to kill, penetrate your heart and lungs, and cause internal bleeding. They hung over my progress that morning like a dark, suffocating cloud. Slowly, my arms turned to lead. Without the occasional flotsam slipping past, or the noise of birds in the air to pull me back from the brink, I slip into these voids of depression like sand through a sieve. I lost it.

What happened next, was something akin to opening a pressure cooker. I started to sing. I just opened my mouth and out they came; The Beatles, Stones, Bob Dylan, even some obscure song from Geno Washington and the Ram Jam Band. If I had been stopped, I would almost certainly have been taken for a fool gone mad, put on medication or even worse, in the insane asylum. Thank God, the spell broke on hearing Grand Bruit's moaning buoy. I swallowed deeply, turned the page on my thoughts of relationships, and hoped that my next brush with insanity would happen on land, close to a bottle of brandy.

The views presented by the Southern Shore were changing slowly. After Couteau Head, the coastal mountains turn inland in quilted patches of brown and red. Eagles were now a common sight, and sometimes scattered caribou foraging on a beach. Near Muddy Hole Point, a majestic, many pointed moose, skulking close to shore, on sensing me, leapt and bounded as if on stilts, into the undergrowth. The sky ahead was bleached off colour, then what I was beginning to take as a normal part of any day, a new easterly front started to blow. It was still between seasons. The only constant since starting, had been the rain. The sun played hide-and-seek and the wind couldn't make up its mind which way to blow. That afternoon, the wind was shifty. The atmospheric forces overhead were gathering their armies. Who really gave a damn who came out on top? Dark clouds are dark clouds, and if one thing was certain, I would get wet.

I had been going point to point all day; Long Point, Otter Point, Muddy Hole Point, Kelpy Point. I was now resting at Barasway Point, debating whether to risk the coming storm and sprint across Barasway Bay to Burgeo, or stay put for the night on this exposed beach. Once again, I had a contact to aim for. A young couple who were into kayaking, lived in Burgeo. They were friends of a friend. I had tapped into that underground network of safe havens that all travelers search for, and I was now being passed down the line like a friendly acquaintance, but should I risk open water at the bottom of the day for the sake of a night indoors?

Again, a night between clean sheets seduced me back on the water, but within the hour I was regretting it. It didn't take long for the bay to wake-up and kick-ass. The wind and rain set in before the halfway mark. I was soon bracing against every other wave. Upwind, the waves looked foreboding. They advanced in dark ranks of breaking faces and shadowy troughs, while downwind, silvery and deceptively calm in shiny crests, they traveled away from me into the bay. It's always the same; battle the elements, or surf them.

As hard as I tried to angle my kayak into the wind, I couldn't keep a steady course. Burgeo was slipping away. I was being pushed into the danger zone of shallow water and heavy surf at the bottom of the bay. I was now paddling on willpower alone, since I'd been on the water for twelve hours and covered nearly forty miles. Once again, I was dipping into an empty well, and once again, it was decision time. Either I could turn with the wind and surf in the near certain knowledge that I would capsize in shallow waters but be swept ashore at the bottom of the bay, or risk angling down the wind to a point of land in deep water, and maybe end up swimming ashore. Both ideas had their strengths and weaknesses, but neither were life threatening. The wind was coming from the sea and the tide was rising.

I was surfing like a schooner under full sail. It was fantastic. Leaning into walls of water, bracing, surging in front of rising waves one minute, being chased by its crested surf the next; but that was the only highlight of the day. I beached under a falling sun, erected my tent under fatigue, near a mosquito infested slew, then lay awake almost all night in a damp sleeping bag.

Fog as thick as pea soup greeted me when I popped my head out of the tent. I hate fog - with a passion! It gives me the willies. It always makes me aware of just how small and insignificant a kayak is, and how easily an unseen noise can appear through the gloom and cut it in two. It makes me feel claustrophobic, see ghosts, and for some strange reason, known only to me - now shared with you the reader - return to my youth.

To this day, I can still remember the infamous week in England during the spring of '58, when everything came to a grinding halt. It wasn't caused by a war, killer plague or the world cup of soccer, it was SMOG. That lethal mixture of fog and fuel smoke that chokes out the sun like a theatre curtain had descended on Great Britain and was seeking permanent residency. I was nine years old at the time.

I was heading home from school. We'd been let out early, warned to stay together in friendly groups and not to take our normal shortcut across a farmer's field. Even in those days, Bernie danced to his own drum. My friends had taken to the pavement while I took the trail across the field.

The smog was into its second week of occupation, but that day had been the worst yet. You could hardy see your hand in front of your face. I'd just let go of a tree and had my eyes fixed as firmly as a train to its tracks, on another, some distance away. I had crossed this field hundreds of times, but of course today was different. I remember getting tired and my concentration wavering. When you are young you're fearless. You have the impudence that only life experience can burn out of you. What I had then, was called false courage. The trail melted into short grass, then later into a pool of mud. I was lost. I remember lying down and looking through an opening in the mist into a clear blue sky and asking the question "Why Me?" I honestly believed that it was God's punishment; for what I don't know. Eventually, I found my way home, but not without having the fright of my life.

Was it Freud or Jesus Christ who said that you have to face your demons? Look them in the eye and say "Begone you Heathens!" Let me tell you, it didn't work in my youth and it doesn't today either.

I did eventually pry myself out of my sleeping bag, take the tent down and paddle off into the gloom...... but I never let go of the land. I now know every inch of beach, face of rock, nest and angry bird from Fox Point to Burgeo. I didn't relax for a minute and it wasn't until a face materialized out of the gloom, like my guardian angel, that I could unwind.

That day, I kissed the land. I thanked my mother for giving me the luck of the Irish, my father for giving me the balls to try, and later, I thanked the Newfoundland Liquor Control Board for supplying the alcohol.

....Never again I thought, but I knew I was lying again.

Chapter: 4
Popeye the Sailor Man

I'm not the young buck I used to be, but what I have lost in speed, I make up for in common sense. There was a time, not long ago, when I would puncture my way through 30 to 40 knot headwinds just for the hell of it, and enjoy the ride. Today, I earn my grey hairs the respectful way, through age, not stage fright. Today, I pick my spots. I get up earlier to beat the wind, and on previous trips, I've also paddled during the night when the winds have died.

I'm not Popeye the Sailor Man, who can turn to spinach whenever his tank gauge reaches empty, but I'm finding the sugar high of Mars Bars a good substitute. All in all, two weeks into my trip, I felt confident, and with yet another night between clean sheets and a belly full of cereal, was more than ready to greet whatever the day would offer.

The morning I left, I was biting at the bit. The sun had risen into a clear blue sky and the sheltered waters around Burgeo were glass calm, but of course, this is Newfoundland. I know this must sound like a worn-out record, but Newfoundland seems to live by its own rules when it comes to forecasting weather. I was beginning to believe that those dark, angry clouds, lurking like pirates down the bays, behind hills and below horizons, those forces of nature that for generations, have humbled, molded and bedeviled both its inhabitants and its visitors, ready to pounce when least expected, were now just waiting for Bernie to dip his paddles into the waters.

I don't think seasonal calenders exist in Newfoundland. June should herald the beginning of summer. Today was June 2nd, yet today's weather would warm me, chill me, wet me, and wait for it...... snow on me! Its reputation for offering four seasons in one day was about to be proved right.

I've seen pictures of longliners gliding across water so

transparent that the sea's bottom is clearly visible. I've watched boats appear to float mystically on a cushion of ether and fearful jagged rocks made visibley smooth through its watery lens. Everything that morning, seemed to come out of the pages of a tourist brochure. The scenes that unfolded in front of my eyes when leaving the harbour, looked to good to be true. It just didn't feel right. It was as though I didn't deserve it. My inner instincts were telling me to skirt the cliffs ahead, follow their contours and stay close to land. Surf would not be a problem. Like icebergs, there was more cliff below water than was visible above. Every escape route today would hold a deep water anchorage. I would be spoiled with choice if the wind picked up. The only danger would come from reflective waves and the occasional confused sea around its inlets. To cross point to point across fifteen miles of open water that morning, seemed a needless risk, but in the open seas around Burgeo, the ceiling had lifted to a brightness like a dawn that I hypnotically followed. My eyes had immediately latched onto an impressive volcano shaped island, and before I knew it, I'd let go of the land and was two miles out in open sea.

The views of the receding shoreline and of the coast ahead were imposing and majestic. White Whale Bay, cut out of vertical rock like a mortal wound, dominated the coast. Dark faces of shadow, sometimes jagged and sometimes smoothed by centuries of storms, rose and fell into the distance like the bared teeth of an angry wolf. Everything that morning, seemed larger than life.

Once past the shelter of Burgeos' myriad of islands, I fell under the influence of yesterday's southeast winds. A sea was on. Once again, I found myself paddling through the ocean's rollercoaster of peaks and valleys. The breathless silence that followed my progress was so inviting that I almost gave into the thought of paddling to Ramea, ten miles out to sea. By midmorning, the Burgeo - Ramea ferry, Gallipilo, had come and gone, then I passed through an armada of fishing boats, out jigging for cod. I was now totally relaxed into a rhythm and eating up the miles.

The pirates struck at noon. Clouds appeared from nowhere, driven by a polar breeze, as they say. It carried a flurry of snow and then turned into rain. The wind didn't pick up until I was within striking distance of Bear Head, but once I had slung-shot around its base, the wind throttled up from medium to strong within minutes.

Reflective waves, confused seas; call them what you want, I was being battered from one wave to the next like a ping-pong ball, swamped and soaked one minute, and freeze-dried by the wind the next. I ate four Mars Bars in one hour, and they did the trick. A burst of energy, a controlled shiver, and I was home and dry........well not quite.

I almost missed Grey River. I had just sprinted past a point of land, was traversing some heavy chop, when I spotted a speedboat. On striking a wave, its small aluminum hull had reared up on its hind end like an excited stallion. The tide was roaring out, and aided by a strong river current, and compressed through a narrow opening in rock, now turned upon itself where it met the sea swell like a river's rapid.

Sometimes your perception plays trick with you, but the opening to Grey River had looked no wider than a hockey rink. The wind had been that strong, my progress that fast and my concentration so intense, that I had missed its beacon above the rock. If I had not seen the speedboat, I most certainly would have missed out on the community of Grey River, and what would turn out to be one of the most unusual sights Newfoundland can offer a person like myself.

Grey River unfolded like the pages of the book. First, I saw its graveyard on the opposite shore, then its wharf, a church steeple, then a neat cluster of utility style of houses, stepping up the side of a hill like colourful paddy fields. I beached at its wharf, spent forty five minutes - still in my damp, cold wet suit - looking for a place to camp. There wasn't an inch of ground or blade of grass that didn't belong to the owner of the window that looked over it. I was very conscious of the fact that if I asked permission to camp in someone's back yard, it would be tantamount to asking for a bed in their home. I dislike the idea of imposing myself on any household, but time was moving on. The sun had already passed behind a backdrop of steep hills. I didn't relish the thought of running the gauntlet back down the inlet to the open sea, and the only other option was to paddle five miles up Grey River to a cove that deadended at Southeast Arm; then I saw it............

One thing you notice on the coastline of Newfoundland, is a lack of cars. It's not that they don't have them. Pick-up trucks are the vehicle of choice; it's just that you don't see the industry that supports them. Petrol stations are on highways, garages are self-made and what is one person's broken-down old banger, is someone else's spare parts. That's not to say you don't see new cars, but they are a rarity. So imagine me, seeing one parked in someone's garden, where no roads exist, and where the maze of community pathways center spaces - between houses - no wider than the car itself. Where did it come from? Why was it here? Did the owner buy it just for status? The mind boggles. I asked these questions of the first person I saw.

"It's not the only one you'll see here. Gerry's also got one in his mother's garden. Been working in Ontario. They didn't want to sell 'em. Been there for a few years. T'was a bugger getting 'em here from t'warf."

Actually, when you think of resettlement, of all those families up-rooting their homes, rafting them over open sea, then planting them back down, it's not hard to imagine these people wanting to store their come-from-away automobiles in their back gardens.

By now, a small group had circled us, and soon the inevitable question, the one that seemed to reach out from a crowd like a friendly hand, came my way.

"Want a cup of tea?"

I ended up being stormbound in Grey River for two days. A gale warning had been posted, but you didn't have to look skywards to read the signs. Even though its inlet was narrow, the sea swells had forced their way through and were rolling past the wharf like lines of storm troopers on parade. The mouth of the river must have looked like the jaws of hell and one could only imagine the angry seas battering the cliffs at its mouth.

I was becoming edgy. I felt like I was imposing on the family I was staying with. They had little space in their small house, so their couch had been my home for two days. I had already emptied my bank of stories and was now starting to crave the privacy of my own tent.

I should have stayed that morning, but I was climbing their walls. I was beginning to feel like a caged tiger. I'd been measuring the cuts in the sky and gauging waves as one does with tidal bores, when I heard a speedboat leave the wharf, en route to the sea.

For the next two days, I fought with the seas, the reason for doing the trip, and my own sanity, but one could never fault the scenery. Without a shadow of doubt, the coastline from Grey River to McCallum was the most impressive I'd ever seen. The cliffs on this section are like huge knuckles of rock, sometimes barren, and sometimes topped by stunted trees, but always cut vertically. Inlets opened as if chiseled from bare rock, and their deep, threatening openings were lost to shadow like dimly lit streets. Fjords cut mountains in two, and everywhere, rock surfaces were streaked with water. Faces wept with surface springs, thundered with waterfalls and everywhere seas boiled under the influence of tremendous tidal surges. If only the weather had cooperated, I could have stopped and explored, but it didn't.

I ended up paddling point to point, two and sometimes three miles out to sea. It's not that I was trying to make up for lost time, or cut corners, it's just that the large sea swells recently produced by the constant southwest winds were more uniform off-shore than in, and the strong, gusting off-shore winds (caused by the funnelling effect that the high walled fjords created) had little influence over my progress two miles out. Throw in *rafting waves* (caused when wind direction and tides are in conflict), *confused seas* (caused when sea currents rise to the surface in shoal water close to shore), and *reflective waves* (caused by sea swells bouncing off solid walls of rock in deep water), and you can understand why I would rather be paddling off-shore than in. Waves out to sea, in deep water, rarely crest with any force in moderate conditions, so aside from having to put up with being tossed about like a ball on a rubber band, my only problem was sea sickness.

It had been my choice all along, to paddle off-shore, but I did miss the close-up views these amazing coastal rock formations offered. The fjords, even at that distance, looked awesome, and their sheltered waters seductive. I also missed my daily chit-chats with the lobster fishermen who trapped close to shore. I'd lost my radio the other day to a beach, so they had become my only source of up-to-date weather information, but just as importantly, news of the Stanley Cup. I had spotted the occasional longliner, out cod fishing, but as everyone on the coast knows, cod fishing licenses are few and far between and the cod even rarer. During a particular bad patch of weather, one sail boat made a detour my way and that night while camped on a beach, my fire had beckoned to a family who were en route home by speedboat to Francois.

Generally speaking, people knew where I was, where I'd been, and except for the general concern one gives to a fellow seaman out in rough seas, the only question I'd been asked so far was....... "Have you seen a good psychiatrist lately?"

At one point, more out of boredom than to take a rest, I turned into the sheltered waters of Richard's Harbour. The cliffs at its entrance echoed to the sounds of crashing waves. Swells came at me from all directions; broadsided from the harbour's inlet, reflected ones came from its cliffs and strange ones from below. Sometimes waves washed over me from behind and sometimes from in front. For five minutes, I paddled, braced and willed my way forward, but no sooner had I entered the inlet, when its seas stretched, yawned and fell asleep.

Chapter: 5
Primary Colours

I had hoped this trip would be full of primary colours; that I would not only find the coastline to my liking, but also its inhabitants, and so far I'd not been disappointed.

I like those easy B plot movies and places that are not sophisticated, civilized, nor cool; places where you can call a spade, a spade without fear of being accosted by the politically correct, or by people who turn gender issues into dogma. Like a bee searches for nectar, I search out isolated communities, preferring to arrive with the sweat of travel still damp on my clothes and wearing a face, not a mask, that reflects the day's conditions. I like to be around people who wave their characters about like flags in the air, and to travel in areas where the smooth crust of life lasts only the length of time it takes to chip its surface. I love the sounds of life, the roars of laughter, shouts of anger, whistles, cat calls, but most of all, the background hum of chatter.

I've been called a hermit and anti-social, which sounds like a contradiction to my love of chatter, but those who see me as a loner, don't really know me. Because of my unusual and solo lifestyle, I've been told that it's easy to become mad from loneliness, lovelessness, or a biological chemical jumble. If so, I'd rather fly with the eagles in the clouds of insanity, than live in medicated streets with the chickens, governed by fear. I wear my oddness like a badge of honour. I've lived with kings and paupers, businessmen and prostitutes, Buddha's and one-eyed street dogs. Take the skin away, and we're all the same underneath. So when I kayaked into David that early evening in McCallum, I knew instantly on meeting his gaze, that I was in the presence of a Buddha.

I had just finished pulling my kayak up its slip-way. I'd already decided to camp on an open patch of stage, between some lobster traps, when a hand the size of a sledge hammer reached out for my own.

"Fine machine, me boy........fine machine."

With lines etched on his face like the contours of a land map, a mouth that opened and closed as if gasping for air, and eyes that at the sight of my kayak, had lit up like those of a child's let loose in a candy store, this man, to the casual observer, must surely have been mad. He was chattering, mostly with himself, but his eyes, transfixed in wonderment with what lay at my feet, told me better than any words, what was on his mind.

You didn't have to be a psychiatrist or social worker to see that the gears of his mind had been stripped long ago. But you needed to live there; you needed to see that this man fit into his environment like a well-worn glove; that whether by birth or accident, this man's naked, childlike emotion hadn't dampened his enthusiasm for life, and that was the only thing that mattered to me.

"Can I paddle her? Can I....? Can I....?"

He was now marching on the spot as if wanting to pee. A small crowd of children was egging him on, in ripples of laughter.

"Can I...? Can I...?

Normally, I'm as protective of my kayak as a cowboy is with his horse. I have this unwritten law that says, you can touch, but you can't paddle. But how could I refuse the gathering crowd, and more to the point, how could I refuse David? They say you have to see into a person's eyes to know their soul. David was unrelenting. His words wrapped around me in a bear hug and his eyes glowed like the warm embers of a fire.

"Have you ever paddled, mate?" I knew the instant my words fell out of my mouth, he'd say yes; that yes really meant no, and that he knew my question was really permission. He wasn't so much digesting my words, as my body language.

Five minutes later, his arms rotating like windmills, going 'round in circles, wearing a smile that slit his face from ear to ear, and laughing like a hyena, David took centre stage in a whirlpool of spray.

There's a fine line between genius and insanity. That night, David and I walked that fine line, as kindred spirits. He followed me around the village like a cat searching for a new home, always in attendance, always ready to tug at my shirt sleeves or flash me a smile. Maybe I reminded him of some long passed-away, favourite uncle or a childhood friend. He took tea with me in other peoples' houses, watched in amazement, as I used the school's internet access to email my friends, and was even instrumental in gaining permission for me to spend the night in McCallum's waterfront Fire Hall. He was the last person I saw that night, and the first person to come knocking at my door as the next day broke.

That night, stripped of all the baggage we explorers carry - of being the most courageous, fastest, strongest, most durable, or of the travel writer who is pressured into compressing chapters into highs and lows - I wrote something for myself, to be posted on my website. Something important, yet insignificant. Something I saw in Burgeo, that David would also have seen and probably shared the same conclusion. It's based on an old Irish saying;

June 6th
A good lie is better than the boring truth.

Did I tell you about Cid from Burgeo? For the sake of this letter and for the sake of Cid's reputation, I will call him Bernardo Franchetti. Bernardo, as the story goes, arrived in these parts from Sicily, under mysterious circumstances, and ever since that day, boots filled with rocks have been turning up on shore.

Cid is your average Joe, except for one small tick. He collects boots. I asked him about the scores of rock-filled boots piled up on his stage, but his answer "To weigh down my nets", wasn't good enough to a city slicker like me. Now, it takes a leap of faith to believe that he buys not any kind of boots, but only ones with rocks in them. What Cid does-

n't know about boots, isn't worth mentioning. The guy is a walking dictionary of waders, poggies, wellies, rubbers and boots. Personally, I like the story that I made up about his Sicilian connection to the Mafia; of feet encased in rock-filled waders, bodies being lobbed overboard during full moon, maggots eating up the evidence, and of time returning Cid's boots back to shore.

I left McCullum the next morning, under a clear blue sky. I paddled past the hill of bare rock under which it sheltered, and the houses that stuck like magnets to its face. I'd enjoyed walking its interconnecting maze of boardwalks, meeting David, making new friends and relaxing into an easy chair of hospitality, bar none. Now, with my back to David and my face towards the sea, that natural loneliness that we all feel on leaving, no matter how independent we are, only intensified. I craved some solace, some words of wisdom and it's at these times I reach for my Bible, the Irish psalm for idiots; the one taped by my knee, inside the cockpit of my kayak, the one that reminds me of the child inside all of us, that we crave to return to:

"When we are young, the summers seem endless, stretched out in the heat and the long days; that paradise before far-off school resumes. But as we grow older, summer has a way of shortening, hurrying and reminding us of how few there may be left."

That morning, Hermitage Bay was becalmed and a light coastal mist shattered its rising sun into a million fragments. I didn't have any marathon ambitions that day, but I knew I had to get a move-on. I had heard from a group of fishermen in McCallum that a storm was just around the corner. The morning weather was deceptive; strong winds were already sweeping across the Avalon Peninsula, and they were supposed to arrive in our region by late afternoon.

I enjoyed the bay's traverse more than all the rest put together. It was predictable and intimate, and for once, the weather was accommodating. Clouds were receding towards the sea's horizon, like tendrils snaking into open blue. It was, as they say on the coast, "A Large Day", full of expectation. It had all the ingredients I like; sun, shade and breeze, with just a hint of mist. A flock of ducks twisted and turned ahead, then banked in formation before skidding to a halt in groups of two's and three's. They were good omens, and as they preened and pruned themselves, I took a bearing on Pass Island and started my lazy eight mile paddle across Hermitage Bay to its eastern shore.

Halfway across, I turned to face the sound of a rising whale. Not fifty feet away, I saw a fin, then as its glistening back arched, ready to submerge, yet another broke the surface. They were rising and falling in unison and heading in my direction. One glided almost to my stern before disappearing in a curl of water, while the other rose not twenty feet away from my bow, sighed, geezered out a shoot of atomized water, then sank back under the surface without evidence of a wake.

How powerfully yet gently these creatures from the deep move through water. It's no wonder they have spawned so many romantic stories, and are the centre of so many mystic tales. I always shrink in their presence. To experience a whale close-up and personal, so unannounced, is akin to being a grounded fly surrounded by elephant feet.

I'd heard numerous whales break surface during this trip, but never seen them so clearly. Almost everyday, I'd seen their spouts and heard the sucking noises they make while swallowing in air. I had been told that they were more numerous on the coastline than the coastal seal, but in rough conditions, almost impossible from my elevation to see.

Further on, I encountered a huge pod of porpoise. I gave up counting them at forty, lost count of times that they shot out of the water, swam under my kayak, and sometimes three abreast, came within spitting distance of my paddle blades.

The mist returned near Pass Island tickle, but no sooner had I stuck my nose into Connaige Bay, when out of the mist, a sailboat materialized. I was awestruck. It was sailing at the whim of a cunning breeze, where I felt none existed. It moved across the sea with the elegant smoothness of a fin through water. I loved its windborne sounds of bells, the twang of its rigging and half empty sails, flapping in search of a breeze. They share with me, a sense of the elements, of being exposed, dwarfed and humbled. It was a converted schooner, all wood and chrome, and as I watched, its sails billowed and filled, then took off at speed on a course to the Burin Peninsula.

The Southern Shore was now behind me. Its sharp peaks and valleys of naked rock now gave way to rolling hills of green. Shallow cliffs tapered down to sandy beaches and everywhere the land was underlined in gold.

As I started my traverse of Connaige Bay, a lobster fisherman dropped by for a chat. He'd reinforced the morning weather forecast, pointed out the dark threatening clouds coming out of the northeast and advised me to take shelter in Harbour Breton. The writing was on the wall, and no sooner had I turned down the bay, when the wind picked up, the waves started to raft, and I was once again sitting in a pool of water.

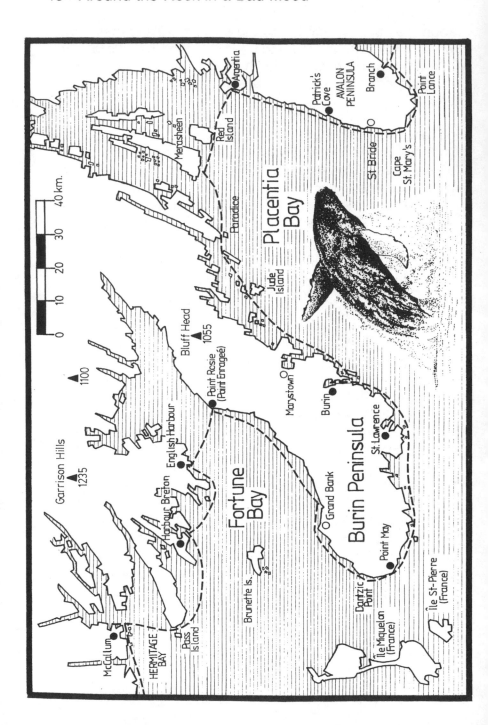

Chapter: 6
No Pain, No Gain

I took this from my website. At that time, my mood swings reflected the weather.

June 5th: Harbour Breton

I am stormbound in Harbour Breton and for once, the weather forecast was spot-on. So far, the Marine Weather Forecast has been as predictable as my daily plans and that's not saying much. I had given up on their predictable wind speeds, and even their directions leave a lot to be desired. The weather forecast, like the radio beacon sea buoys and unmanned lighthouses, are geared towards the off-shore dragging fleets and merchant shipping. We coastal inshore users are their poor cousins. You can't blame them, back in HQ, for discounting the poor lobster fisherman or the coastal longliners out fishing cod. We are too close to land and too few in number to count, and that's why I ask for local information whenever possible.

Newfoundlanders are a breed unto themselves. They have a rare genius for place names that advertise local conditions. Take for instance, the two Blow-me-Downs between Francoise and McCallum; they really did blow me down. Then, there are the dangerous waters around the aptly named, Wrecks Cove, near Burgeo. And Cape Spear, further down the coast, doesn't exactly sound welcoming. Points of land, high hills and deep bays seem to manufacture their own local conditions and you can't beat it when you hear of these little quirks of nature from the locals who have to live by the side of them. But, and this is a large but, when the Marine Weather Forecast calls for a Gale Warning, everyone listens.

Today it's that windy, I dare not even leave my tent, in case it takes off for the mainland. My pegs are history. They left the ground during the first hour and now, all that keeps the tent from being airborne, is me.

The gale arrived just after dawn and hasn't abated yet. The noise has been deafening. Between the constant flapping noises of my fly-sheet beating on my tent, the constant whine of the wind, and the rapping of the rain at my door, the day is turning out to be a lesson in patience.

Sometime in the morning, I stepped into a pool of water. That's not a big deal; a wet foot here or there wouldn't bother anyone, but in my tent, it's another story. I had conveniently camped in a hollow that was now rapidly filling. I spent the next hour using my towel as a sponge, but no sooner had I sponged one pool dry, when another would form. Then I found the problem. The water was being blown in through a tear in the side of the tent.

The whole situation was laughable, but when the wind changed direction in the early evening and blew my vestibule-cum-fly-sheet on top of my tent and threatened lift-off, I wanted to cry........is there anybody up there?

It rained continuously for almost thirty hours and when I woke into my second morning, shrouded in fog, I turned over, stuck a munchy in my mouth and ate it before falling back into sleep.

Thank God I've learned the value of patience. I woke again under a dome of perfect blue. The fog hung like curtains over the hills and made a perfect halo around the rising sun, but the waters shimmered and winked. Everything looked inviting, but hidden away in the armpit of a deadend inlet behind the community, I had no way of knowing what the conditions were like in open sea. The fog burned rapidly, but the open window view it gave me an hour later, didn't look good. The evidence of a strong wind could be read in the torn clouds, flying inland. They were peeling away from each other like damp paper from a wall; not a good sign, but I left anyway.

Everything went smoothly, up until the point when I turned the corner at Western Head and started to paddle over to its eastern brother. Without warning, the sky turned white. A squall of mist and wind hit me like a wall of snow. It ripped the paddle from my hands, tore my cap from my head and gave my kayak wings. It was like paddling through a wind tunnel. The two arms of rock, that only moments before had stretched out so invitingly towards the sea, now folded to shut down my progress. In less than twenty minutes, the wind and current had combined to throw me back almost a mile.

It's never dangerous paddling into headwinds, but it's punishing on your body. I would have been crazy to continue. I knew the wind was only localized. It caused no sea swell, wasn't cold and carried little punch. It was probably fueled by a falling sun and fanned and funneled by the action of the cool, early evening air rubbing up against the hot, radiantly heated bald surfaces of rock that guarded the inlet. They're called afternoon blows, only lasting the time it takes for the sun to set into dusk, and it was with that thought in mind, that I beached, put up my tent on a ledge carpeted in moss, then laid down inside to wait out the wind.

I love kayaking at night, when the wind has died and the sea is sleeping. It's great to have that feeling of being alone, of having it all to myself. The feeling that a damp evening chill gives to your body is invigorating, as are the sounds of my own breath and the rhythmic lapping noises that my kayak makes cutting through water. I like watching the stars coming out and losing myself to the Milky Way. It's fun to shock the occasional fisherman out jigging, or a couple out copulating. The chatter of ducks, the haunting call of loons, the distant throbbing of some longliner's engines returning home are soothing sounds, but most of all, I like the sea's spectacular light show of the ocean's nocturnal gift called plankton.

The Northern seas are teaming with plankton and all you have to do is disturb them, and they light up like stardust in a night sky; paddle strokes swirl in sparkles of light and bow waves taper off like illuminated sea snakes; fish shoot by like white-hot tracer bullets; whales rise and fall in mushrooms of light, and surprised seals in depth charges that flash and crack.

I set off into a setting sun towards St. John's Head and rounded it en route to English Harbour, as dusk settled into night. Crossing point to point during the dusk was easy, but that night, there was no moon. By St. John's Island, everything had turned ink black, and it wasn't until I latched onto English Harbour's illuminated buoy, that I felt I could relax.

"No pain, no gain," my mother used to say, and today I earned my stripes the hard way. The day started on a bad note, then went to good, very good, then to very, very bad within the space of only four hours. What a rollercoaster.

Morning found me camped out and shivering on a fishing stage. I had woken into a conversation. My tent had surprised two fishermen, and my waxy appearance, as I stepped out to greet them, only made matters worse. It wasn't the night's paddle that had hollowed my cheeks and burned away my colour, it was my wet suit. I had been so tired after putting up my tent, that I had forgotten to strip-off and change. I must have shivered a kilogram of weight away. One of the guys jokingly mentioned the holocaust, and the other, his sister's diet. They took pity on me immediately, stoked up the stove in their fishing shed, made me a coffee, shared their sandwiches, then double-checked the day's forecast for me, before leaving to check out their lobster traps.

Fortune Bay was serene. Light winds skittered over its surface, wrinkling its waters in circular barepods of motion, but the picture was misleading. Apparently, the heavy winds that had storm-bound me in Harbour Breton, were about to make a U-turn.

Just as with the crossing of Hermitage Bay, I was looking for omens. I did spot a group of playful ducks in the harbour, and the point of land I would be heading towards, seemed to be nestled between two dark, yet courtable bosoms. It wasn't the view that morning that rang my alarm bells, or the threatened storm, it was the name of the point of land that I would be taking compass readings from. Its name was Point Enrageé, French for angry point, and that morning, it lived up to its name.

I had woken at 5:00 am, after a mere two hours' sleep. There were still cobwebs in my eyes and even after I'd thawed out, dried my clothes and finished a filling breakfast of sandwiches, I still felt weak. At that moment, the thought of a fifteen mile crossing of open water or an impending storm, wasn't my major worry.

When the seas are glass calm, like they were that morning, and the sun is all glare, it's easy to get listless, give in to fatigue and in my case, sleep. The only difference between my symptoms and those of a truck driver, is that if he fell prey to sleep, he would likely take someone with him, whilst I would pass through the Pearly Gates on my own. With no clear points of land to aim for, no buoys or noticeable traffic for my eyes to latch onto, it's easy to fall into the delusionary state that tells the brain, "you are going nowhere fast."

I know that I should have stayed. English Harbour was a perfect spot to wait out a storm. The fishermen had offered me their fishing shed for the duration; it had a room with a view, a piping hot stove and there was ample room to bed down. Since I was already ahead of schedule, one more day here or there on land wouldn't make any difference. I am not goal orientated. I don't care if I paddle ten miles one day and thirty miles the next. It's just that I had found a rhythm; one that saw me on the water at 7:00 am and found me on shore by 7:00 pm. Routines and rhythms are hard to gain at the beginning of any trip, and easily lost. I had found mine on the Southern Shore, and I didn't want to lose it.

I was in the water and paddling by 7:00 am, but by 9:00 am, I was worried. I wasn't even halfway across Fortune Bay. Without the occasional flotsam slipping past, there was no immediate way to determine speed or distance, or if I was moving at all. The water was mesmerizing. All I had to go by, was the steady, snake-like wake that tailed behind my kayak. Yes, it was hot, and my head felt fried. Past experience told me to sprint for shore, but that was easier said than done. This was the kind of day to put in some good numbers, latch onto faraway points of land and reel myself towards them, but the heat haze had taken away my pulleys. That invisible chord that had served me so well, the one running between whatever my eyes chose to focus on and my kayak, was nowhere to be found. I was drifting aimlessly, not in the sea, but in my mind, and if I couldn't regain concentration, I could be out there all day. Then a breeze picked up. Suddenly, the jigsaw puzzle in my head fell into place, and my rhythm returned

By 11:00 am, I was closing in on the far shore, but had misjudged the bay's current. Almost five miles from my goal and two miles from shore, I was still three miles back down the bay. I was already paddling into a stiff breeze, and as I closed in on the land, lost sight of Point Enrageé. Now, I was grinding on, more out of pride than any need to make mileage. The airborne spray from the rafting waves that I was ploughing through, had already whitewashed my hands. Once again, my bottom was waterlogged, and I was beginning to get cold, very cold.

The last few miles were done at a snail's pace. The wind was screaming down the bay and I was now navigating one of those unforgiving shorelines that hold little shelter, either from wind or wave. Whipped up by the strong cornering winds, the waves were both steep and pointed. My kayak plunged into them repeatedly. One moment I would be stopped dead in my tracks, water would splash into my lap, then my next paddle stroke would get me moving again. Sometimes strokes hit dead air; I would twist, be broadsided, then have to spend the next few minutes straightening her out again. Whenever I am asked about kayaking, and its dangers, I always stress these periods. For me, they always seem to occur at the end of the day, within sight of the finish line, when my fuel gauge reads near empty. It's at these times, at the very height of the battle, when you're sucked into its vortex, that I take a time out, and today was no exception. I stopped paddling, allowed the wind and waves to push me back, reached down into my cockpit, poured myself a thermos cup of coffee, lit a cigarette and chilled out.

I don't know what it is that lifts me the most; the caffeine, the nicotine, or my actions that poke a finger at the conditions, but once the exercise is finished, even though the elements may have pushed me one mile back, I always manage to close the gap between myself and the finish line in no time.

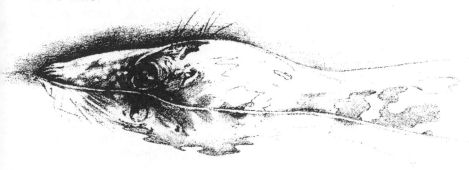

Chapter: 7
Lean, Mean, Paddling Machine

It seams that no matter how careful I am during the day, some wave will force its way through the protective cockpit skirt I wear (just for that reason) and end up puddling in my seat. Inevitably, I will end the day sitting in a pool of cold sea water. I have tried everything from duct taping the skirt to my waist to seal it, to tightening up the cord that secures the skirt to the cockpit so tightly to its frame that if I capsized, I would have a hard time getting out. In short, I am just about glued in, but nothing seems to work. Just the other day, I thought I got away with a dry one, then I got a call from nature. There I was, holding onto my best friend, hanging it over the side, pointing its jet downwind, when an errant wave slapped me.

All things considered, it felt good to be back in the kayak. I was stormbound in Point Rose for three days and the first went well. A family took pity on me and offered a bed. I spent the second day recovering from the first day's hangover and the third, laid up like a beached walrus after a huge traditional Sunday dinner of moose, salt pork, potatoes, cabbage, carrots, turnip, peas and gravy, but the highlight of my stay came on my last night, via the airways.

John Drake, aka CB Singer, was front and centre in his own road show. His open-line starts at 10:00 pm on channel 10. The guy is both announcer and moderator, politician and saint, and going by some of the juicy requests, principal guardian of every known gossip this side of the Avalon Peninsula. His brand of live singing, accompanied by his guitar, has made him a legend in his own lifetime. He's Newfoundland's answer to Ontario's Gordon Lightfoot. You won't find his program advertised in the St. John's Herald, or announced on C.B.C. radio. He's a people-person, a man of all seasons. He treats his listeners as he would his own family, and will sing on request; anything from sea shanti to pop, from pub-style sing-a-longs to a lover's lament. He may be just the lighthouse keeper at St. Jack's Island in Fortune Bay, but if he ever turned his hand to politics, I know one vote he would definitely get.

I was now closing in on Dantzic Point. Jokingly, someone told me that its shoreline vied with Portage and Main as the windiest point in Canada. My Maritime Weather Guide even dedicates a whole page it.

"Strong south easterlies are funneled between the Miquelon Islands and the southwest tip of the Burin Peninsula. This effect enhanced by cornering near Dantzic Point which creates strong winds in this area."

It seems that this stretch of coastline was not only famous for its rum and tobacco smuggling, but for the winds it creates between the mainland and the French protectorate of St-Pierre and Miquelon.

I woke at the crack of dawn to beat these winds. The night before, I had camped just outside Fortune, the last community before the long twelve-mile paddle to Dantzic Point. All night, the gulls had kept me awake. The caplin were coming ashore to spawn and the gulls must have been having a rare feast day. I wasn't really in a fit state to do anything, let alone paddle because I probably had only four hours' sleep if that. It was 4:30 am and freezing cold. Still dark outside, Fortune Bay was tranquil. I was in the water and paddling by 6:00 am, but no sooner had I turned the corner at Fortune Head, when a stiff breeze picked up, then the tide also turned against me.

Getting to Dantzic Point was like climbing a mountain full of false peaks. The point just wouldn't come towards me. The headwind was brutal and relentless. I only stopped once for a coffee break, but the site of land reversing itself at a jogging speed, made for a quick pit-stop. I dug my heels in for eight hours and refused to stop. The whole day went by in slow motion. The wind wore me down like a soapstone and the tide took care of the rest, so when I

eventually turned the corner into Placentia Bay and rounded the point, I was spent. I had been on automatic pilot for
the last two hours, and when I rounded Point May, I threw
in the towel at the first signs of life.

I was that tired, I got swamped surfing ashore, then one
foot tripped over the other, exiting the kayak on the beach,
and I fell. I was now not only tired, but cold and soaking wet.

It's at these moments that life shows me its silver lining.
I had been spotted coming ashore, and once I had picked
myself up, I came face to face with what looked like a
retired member of the Hells Angels. Sitting astride his ATV
as if he owned the place, Mike immediately took me under
his wing, or should I say on top of his ATV. Thirty minutes
later, I was stripped and changed and chewing my way
through a plateful of sandwiches, and later that evening, I
was treated to a three course meal at his cousins. Needless
to say, that evening found me tucked away between clean
sheets. Once again, Newfoundland hospitality had picked
me up after its elements had flattened me.

What a difference a day makes. The morning sun was
on fire, and the sea reflected its rays in flashing ripples, like
a visual morse code.

From Point May to Lawn Bay, it is as if someone had taken a rolling pin to the land. In places it's as flat as a pancake. Low-lying islands and points of land melted into one. Summer had finally arrived and my body at last, had turned into the lean, mean, paddling machine of old. Earlier aches and pains that had marked my mornings were gone. I now felt like I could paddle all day, no matter what the circumstances, and today I wanted to post up some big numbers.

The beauty ahead was unreal. I could see the hazy shadow that I took to be Lawn Head and beyond, the fainter but higher Chapeau Rouge. Open spaces of reflection entranced me, and always, the rhythmic sounds of rushing water over pebbles, followed my progress close to shore. Here and there, patchwork quilts of blues and yellows fought for life and you couldn't beat their ever-present corridors of flowery scent. For the first time, mosquitoes chased me from a beach, and did I feel a bite from the dreaded black fly?

That morning, the sun anaesthetised my back, peeled the clothes off my body and gave me more than a Newfie blush. For the first time since leaving Corner Brook, I could relax into the easy chair of travel, exploring the coastline's nooks and crannies without fear of being swamped. Sea swells heaved and sighed 'round deep-water points of land, but never clapped or crested. Shallow shoals rose up to kiss me and the abundance of spawning caplin, clouded under my kayak like a thousand silver strips, fluttering in the breeze. I saw my first humpback whale roar out of the water and over a score of seals, with their periscope snouts glistening in the sun. The sea and sky were alive to the sights and sounds of the hunter, and caplin was the bait.

I made camp that night at the bottom of Shoal Cove, within stricking distance of St. Lawrence. It was one of the finest beaches I'd seen so far, but the next day only got better.

For the novice kayaker, I would say that the section from St. Lawrence to Jude Island is the most kayaking-friendly waters I had paddled so far. It had a little of everything; inviting coves, impressive cliffs, islands dotting the landscape, enough shoal water to keep you on your toes, and plenty of escape routes to take if the weather turned ugly. Bald eagles were a common sight, whales and seals were everywhere, and there was always plenty of lobster fishermen to pass the time of day with, if you wish...... as well as others!!!

Now, I know that it isn't every child's dream, especially in Newfoundland, to grow up to become a Fish and Wild Life Officer. Uniforms on the coast, whether Provincial or Federal, don't hold the glamour of old. Women don't exactly beat paths to their doors, whether for dates or marriage. Since the cod moratorium, the lime-green uniforms of Newfoundland's Fish and Wild Life Officers have been getting a bad rap. Self-policing on the Rock flew out of the window after Union with Canada; now big brother's tentacles are everywhere.

There is a saying, that you can't even piss on the coast without some federal government official asking to see your permit or to fill in a form, so you can imagine my surprise at being glad to be stopped by two youthful looking Fish and Wild Life Officers. They were quite literally, still under warranty, wearing the smartest command style uniforms I've ever seen. What a sight the duo made. Covered in zips and velcro pockets, with loops holding torches, notebooks at the ready, supporting telephones, and for all I know, grappling hooks and rocket launchers. They wouldn't have looked out of place at a punk rockers' street party. Was I hallucinating? I half expected - when they powered towards me, all jet and surf, like some hot-rod on wheels - that I was going to be fined for not wearing my seatbelt. How wrong could I be.

Chad Ward and Barry Grandy were all smiles. They not only knew who I was, where I was going, but where I was to sleep that night. I had not even introduced myself, when without question on my part and unhesitatingly on theirs, they radioed ahead to warn my host Richard Chisholm, in Lewin's Cove, down Burin Inlet, of my impending arrival. Now if that isn't hospitality, I don't know what is.

I spent two nights and one glorious day of R & R with

Richard and his wife, Cindy. I slept-in, pigged-out on home-made food, updated my website, wrote and posted a dozen postcards, and in the evenings, hovered around the TV remote like a hungry vulture. I slipped into their family routine with the ease of a close friend, but one day is enough when you've miles to go.

I left Burin Inlet under fog. It coiled around trees and blotted out the sun. Needless to say, I got lost. The milky stare of fog that greeted me at Burin Island was unsettling, and the muffled sounds worrisome. Even though the chance of encountering a longliner was probably close to nil, I felt a knot in my stomach as I let go of land and let the cool, moist arms of fog embrace me. For two hours, I slowly picked my way down the coast, more by luck than good judgement. My ears were open to the slightest sounds, and my eyes were forever watchful. Never good at using a compass, I was always stopping to check its needle. The fog was as dense as cotton wool. It was mid-June, but autumn was in the air.

By midmorning, the fog was lifting fairly regularly, but was always punctured by rain. At one point, the land fell away into Mortier Bay. A longliner, obviously en route to the port of Marystown, almost sliced me in two, then another, then another. I was shell-shocked. It was like being caught out on a freeway, like a cat scurrying between wheels. It was becoming impossible to judge speed or distance. The longliners seemed to hover in the mist, as if waiting for the green light, then tear past. At Skiffsail Point, I glued myself to its rock as if my life depended on it. I now paddled on, with the sounds of surf on rocks to guide me, while colourful puffins flew in and out of the mist like guided missiles.

I pulled in at Rock Harbour, ready to call it quits, but no sooner had I turned my back on the water, when the sun popped out. It was not even midmorning, and I was bathed in sweat. My knuckles were purple, my wrist and face, cherry brown, but inside my wet suit, lay a furnace. I used my pit-stop wisely. I stripped and changed, put on my shorts, exchanged my kinky latex cat suit-cum-wet-suit for cotton and wool, and continued.

So far, I had a love-hate relationship with Placentia Bay. She was turning into a proper little seductress. It has pleasing curves, beautiful exposed thighs, and mysterious ankles, shrouded in mist. It had enough character to keep me honest, but where were her passionate currents that I had heard flowed through her veins?

That night found me camped out under the stars, roasting my buns on an open fire. I was tucked-in on a beautiful sand and pebbled cove on Oderin Island, halfway down Placentia Bay and one-third across. I was relaxing into the silence and thinking about the day's paddle ahead. I had planned it that way. The island would be the first of three stepping stones I would use while traversing the bay. I had put a lot of time and effort into asking, listening and digesting information about its waters. On a map, Placentia Bay looks like a crocodile's yawn. Its mouth is so wide, it's easy to spot the location of its jagged teeth, yet it's just as easy to get lulled into overlooking its molars, thinking them blunt and safe. It's easy to be mislead into feelings of safety so far down the bay, away from open sea. It's also easy to forget that when the tide is falling, it not only empties its mouth, but its belly as well, and it's between its molars that you find the veins that the bay's strong, passionate currents pass through.

If the bay's teeth grow on the Avalon and Burin Peninsulas, then it can be said that its protective molars are the islands of Merasheen and Red Island, that guard its throat. When the tide is falling, the currents between these islands are deadly. These passionate currents that flow between these islands and the mainland also have names; Western Channel, Central Channel, and Eastern Channel.

I left the next morning at the break of dawn and made the picturesque summer settlement of Great Paradise in double-quick time. On entry, I had been spotted by a group of playful children, one thing led to another, and by noon, I was sitting down, eating a Sunday dinner with their family.

By midafternoon, I had decided to leave. My hosts had forewarned me about the tidal currents ahead, but there was hardly a cloud in the sky, and there was only a hint of a ripple where the tidal rips should have been. In fact, I was so confident, I had altered my plans to visit Merasheen Island, and instead set a diagonal course to Red Island - some sixteen miles of open sea away - but two miles into my paddle, I had a quick change of plan.

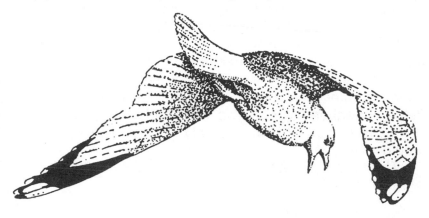

The tide had changed and was in conflict with the wind. I now found myself in a tidal rip. Waves were starting to get choppy, to clap and crest. I had heard that the tides were as strong as a river's current, and now I knew they hadn't been joking. At first, I wasn't worried. Normally these tidal rips are a couple of hundred yards wide at best, but this one went on forever, and to make matters worse, it took me over White Sail Bank - a place where the sea bottom rises from over 100 fathoms to less than 10 fathoms, forcing powerful currents to the surface. It's not that I haven't experienced waters like these before, but I had never been caught out in them for such a long time.

It took three hours to paddle my way through, and another two to get to Merasheen Island, and so ended another day at the office, slightly more humble than when I'd started it.

Chapter: 8
Coming Home

God, I don't believe it........! A dune buggy. What would Joey Smallwood think? That old saying "what goes around comes around" couldn't have been penned better to express the new resettlement program. Don't get me wrong; when I say resettlement, I mean returning back or as they call it out here "Coming Home".

Some of these islands have achieved in the last decade, a kind of renaissance, through summer havens for prior residents. Some distant relatives, who left for the mainland after resettlement, to work in the rich gas and oil fields of northern Alberta and Fort McMurray in particular, have built homes that even the middle classes of St. John's would envy.

This is an excerpt taken from my website on this subject of resettlement;

June 21st
What goes around, comes around.

What would Joey Smallwood say if he could come back and see these new home-away-from-homes? To date, I have visited four old communities that were part of Joey's resettlement program in the early sixties. Whatever your view, and they are many on the Rock, one doesn't have to look far to see that traffic is heading back to the once deserted outports. I have stayed and visited in Point Rose in Fortune Bay, Oderin, Great Paradise and now, Merasheen in Placentia Bay. These outports, their land and their views are up for grabs. I have seen and been in homes more fitted for city life, than roughing it. Long gone are the lantern lights of old. Today, diesel generators are the norm and many have all the luxuries of home and then some. It is true that most are rustic at best and are still inhabited by lobster and cod fishermen who prefer to be close to their fishing grounds and rear their children up in the traditional way, but many more are being renovated or rebuilt for the rich or those who want to return to their roots, albeit just for those lazy, long weekends during summer.

I came to Newfoundland with an open mind. I have travelled enough over the years to not believe all one reads in the newspapers, and never to base one's views on political hearsay. Crab fishermen are the new rich of the Newfoundland fisheries, and those lucky enough to have been granted licenses and went into the industry before it boomed, now have a license to print money. All those who put their eggs into one basket called the Cod and didn't diversify into crab, shrimp and what was once called bi-products, got hit the hardest when the fish moratorium hammer fell. The fishermen who I have spoken to, all enjoyed their work; not the cold reality of waking up at the break of dawn, or the sometimes back-breaking twenty hour, non-stop work schedules they sometimes have between storms, but they enjoy the independence of being their own boss.

But let's get back to the outports. There is a new word - well it was to me called COMING HOME parties. Great Paradise had one recently. I'd been told over 1000 people attended their week-long get together; and for a place with just twenty or so houses, it boggles the mind where all those visitors stayed. People, I had been told, came from as far away as Europe and the States. They all had either been born there, or had been related in some way or another to a person who had. This year, it will be Merasheen's crack at the whip, and they were expecting a thousand visitors also.

I only stayed one night in Merasheen. I was a little gun-shy about leaving after yesterday's bad conditions. The weather was far from ideal, but for me, there's no better medication than getting back in the saddle.

The day wasn't exactly a disaster, but it was sure choker-block full with incident. Middle Channel lived up to its reputation. The wind and tide were in conflict and its waters confused and full of surf. The sky was filled with racing clouds and when they darkened and dived into windborne rain, I took shelter behind Red Island's Hole-in-the-Wall Point.

When the weather is dirty and cold, it can take the heart out of anyone. Red Island looked like the Rock of Gibraltar. It jutted out of the sea like an angry fist. Any other day, I would have beached and explored her, but that morning, it never entered my head. I was gathering my strength, psyching myself up for one final push across the Eastern Channel. I was hoping, no, praying for a window of opportunity. The sea crawled with maggots of surf as if seething in a broad wound. Surf tipped every swell, and the rain was unrelenting. I was of two minds; drop my tail and search out a campsite, or bite the bullet and continue. It's not that the waves were dangerous; I'd been out in worse. No, I was getting cold. I was now working on the principle of 'movement equals heat,' and with that thought in mind, pushed-off.

I got broadsided and swamped on numerous occasions while crossing the channel. The rain had abated, but the sun never came out. Close to shore, the wind took off and took away my intended landing in Placentia, so I ended up beaching on a construction site, under restricted notices around Argentia Peninsula's airport. I was too tired to care, too hypothermic at that moment, to do anything more than light a fire to warm myself. I lit it close to some bushes to gain some shelter from the wind, bordered it with rocks, then took off, walking towards a building site, more from a need to get my blood circulating, than to ask for permission to stay. The last hundred yards from bush to camp were the coldest steps that I have ever taken. Stripped naked, I would have been warmer. I was a prisoner to my wet suit, and what heat I'd gained during the walk, was instantly stolen by a strong wind.

I greeted the first person I saw, as if saved from a hangman's noose, but the sudden change from cold to hot was too much. The canteen's heat ignited a fit of shakes. My teeth chattered uncontrollably and my fingers ached as if squeezed in a vice. Both my index fingers snapped in and out of usefulness, like a faulty transmission, and the soles of my feet cramped like the curved-down surfaces of a shoe. To say I had overdone it, was putting it mildly.

I stayed much longer than I had intended. It was like living a dream. I drank, ate mountains of food in their canteen and used their dryer, then.........

"SMOKE, SMOKE... Where's your camp?"

I'd started a forest fire, well not quite on that scale. Argentia's Emergency Fire Service met us at the scene. We'd already put it out, but they drowned it, just in case. I had expected a reprimand; at the very least, a pack-your-bags-and-go, but this is Newfoundland. When they saw my kayak and heard my story, I was not only treated like the second coming of Lazarus, but later that evening, two crew members dropped by with a cooked supper, Yeh Boy!

From a map, the Avalon Peninsula looks like a plate that has been dropped onto a hard floor; it is fractured into a thousand pieces, forming deep bays, seas within seas, scorpion-tailed peninsula and long, inviting arms of land. I was now paddling the shores of its southeast arm, towards Cape St. Mary's. I didn't want a repeat performance of yesterday's folly, so I plugged away, close to land, never straying out of calling distance from the shore, but something was missing.........boats.

It had been my experience, that fish camps on the coast accumulate like particles of sand 'round bays, coves and inlets. They had been both reassuring and sad sights. I had seen many since leaving Corner Brook, but most were deserted, no more so than today. I only wish I could have circumnavigated the Rock thirty years ago, when cod stocks were abundant and the inshore fisheries still thrived. I would have loved to see beaches filled with playing children, chit-chat daily with people, and breath air filled with the smells of freshly caught fish. Resettlement not only effected the outports, those romantic yet sometimes bleak islands, but also those on the mainland, connected by road.

The Avalon Peninsula has been reduced from a thriving cottage industry of small family fisheries, to a couple of year-round harbours at St. Bride's and Branch. The sixties not only carried with them the germ of T.B., but a slump in cod; despair on despair. People left the small communities like water rushing downhill to places like St. John's and Argentia. The flow from small to large communities started long before Joey Smallwood put pen to paper, gave a name to its reality and called it resettlement. Maybe if he hadn't, the vacant holes would have sealed themselves, but that's history, and at that moment, just a daydream.

If Dantzic Point is Placentia Bay's western gateway, then Cape St. May's is it's eastern counterpart. I had paddled from Argentia to Patrick's Cove, some thirty miles down the coast, to be within shooting distance of the cape. I'd heard many things about Cape St. Mary's, and aside from its world-famous bird sanctuary, none had been good. A quick look at my sea chart was enough to give me a sleepless night.

The cape fragments into three jagged edges. I was told it had riptides, dangerous shoal waters, was a place where the Labrador current and Atlantic collided, and because of its unlimited southwesterly exposure, when the sea was on, wasn't worth trying to round unless you gave it a three mile berth. In fact, I was so worried, I even called into St. Bride's harbour (five miles from the cape) to get a second opinion on the weather, before trying to 'round it, but all was fine.

Holy chit! Before that day, the closest I had been to a duck, was when they had been served to me on a plate, but that was yesterday. What I saw rounding the cape that day, was incredible, thousands of them. I had never seen so many ducks in one place. They were scooters, murres, puffins, guillemots, eider and high above me, a lone bald eagle, getting the hell pestered out of him. At one point, I sat back and drifted through a huge flock of eider ducks. It was like watching a wildlife program in 3-D with surround sound. Some came right up to the kayak, while others, none too interested in my presence, didn't even bother giving me a second glance.

Above, the scene was something akin to Toronto's 401 highway in rush-hour. Birds and ducks were flying everywhere. Whoever is entrusted with air traffic control around here, must have a mega headache, but the best was yet to come; for it wasn't until I had rounded Cape St. Mary's, passed under its lighthouse and saw the False Cape ahead, that I paddled into the main event.

The whole cliff looked like a pin cushion of thousands of white dots. I now recognized the famous picture-postcard scene that bird lovers from around the world come to see. The noise was deafening and no sooner was I spotted, when it got even louder. Literally, hundreds of gannets peeled off the cliff's face and started to swarm over my head. It was a fabulous experience. I was the centrepiece of the action, and for fifteen minutes, had a front-row seat to events above and around me, as they unfolded.

I have my own theory about why thousands of gannets choose this spot, year in and year out, to nest. First, you can't beat the view, but more importantly to the gannet, if you miss your breakfast in the Labrador Current, you can always catch lunch in the Atlantic one just round the corner.

For the more scientific reader, Cape St. Mary's is a place where the warmer Gulf Stream collides with the chilled Labrador Current. It's here that waters cross-hatch in invisible, complex layers of arctic and tropic waters; waves foam under the surface with bacteria, yeast, diatoms, fungi, algae - all the stuff of life that urges growth.

The experience at Cape St. Mary's is up there with the best of them. I am not a bird lover at the best of times, but I could not help but be amazed with what I saw. It will be a moment to savour long after the trip is finished, and the only drawback to the day, was leaving it behind.

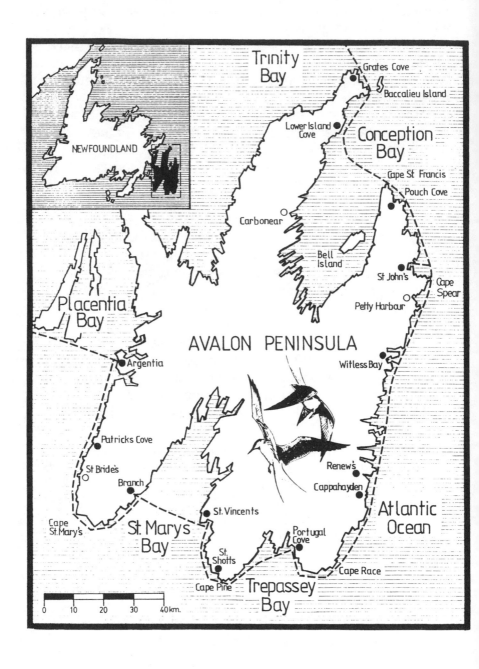

Chapter: 9
Brutal Weather but Fantastic Hospitality

"Fee fee, fi fi, fo fo, fum, I smell the blood of an English man." Do I have Englishman tattooed on my head, or is it my lumbering gate? This captain not only liked Englishmen, but loved them, adorned his bridge with pictures of the Queen, and no doubt, Princes Di, in his bedroom.

"Na let me put it this way", he started to say........but I'm getting ahead of myself.

Once again, I was stuck. I was neither stormbound by wind or by fog. This time, it was a hangover. I was in Branch, a fishing community in St. Mary's Bay, on the west side of the Avalon Peninsula, just down from the cape. The day before, I had tried the twelve mile crossing to St. Vincent's but one mile out, had turned tail, lost in fog and come back.

That was yesterday; today was a different story. The foundation of my present state, started around ten o'clock last night. I was trying to sleep, when a crab boat chugged into the harbour. I had camped opposite the wharf, and the noise they made while unloading their catch, was just too much to take. Eventually, curiosity got the better of me. I went to see what the fuss was about.

"Where's you from boy"?

It was as easy as that. I didn't really need to reply. My accent gave me away and the rest, so they say, is history.

First, I was given the guided tour of his boat, next he checked the 24 hour weather station, then it was down to the serious business of drinking. I have already said that a good lie is better than the boring truth, and you'd better believe me when I say that I can tell a good story, but I was in the presence of a master, one with time to kill and a sea chest full of stories to tell.

What this captain didn't know about fishing, wasn't worth writing home about, and to say it was in his blood, would be a valid truism. This man could trace his family tree back to the 'White Cliffs of Dover'. The term, Canadian, was as distasteful to him as calling an Eskimo a nigger, but he did love the sea, and that language knows no barriers.

What is it about fishing, that ties some people to the sea? It seems the harder the forces of man and nature pull them to leave, the tighter the knot that makes them stay becomes. Maybe it is something as simple as the scent of sea air. I've heard many reasons put forward on this subject, some far-fetched, but that night's conversation on this very subject, struck a chord.

"Why do I keep fishing? That's an easy one," he replied to my question. "It's like opening a present, everytime you haul up the net. You never know what your gonna find, if it'll make ya rich or send ya to the poor house." Maybe this view was some incurable disease handed down in gene pools, from one generation to the next. Maybe the adrenaline rush, of feast or famine, has made them all junkies. Maybe one generation's poison is the next generation's elixir of life. He told me that his father worked on the land, never spending one night on the sea. So maybe it skips generations, like hair loss to a bald man - who knows, but it did seem plausible.

By midnight, the walls were starting to implode, but the more we drank, the more he talked. He had so many untold stories in his head that they seemed to branch off like twisted roots; storms, drowning, fish quotas, and of course, confederation. He unwound before my eyes, like a spring under tension. Stories lay unfinished, like limp threads at my feet, as no sooner had he taken off in one direction, he changed, but who cared? By 2:00 am, he had opened another 12 ounce bottle of rum and that's when I called it a night.

How many times can one clean and repair one's gear, visit newfound friends and build up one's stock of fat? I was now into my third day in Branch. I was becoming a permanent fixture in the boys' room - an empty garage, complete with chairs and a cooler, and open to the sea. It doubled as the unofficial village drop-in centre; a magnet for both the unemployed and retired alike. I revelled in their stories, their good humoured leg-pulling, but mostly, of them, and where else, I asked myself, could I walk into a kitchen unannounced, and within minutes, be offered tea?

Tea is not just the beverage of choice in Newfoundland, but is as fundamental to kitchen life, as prayer is to houses of religious worship. It's served at births, marriages, and is the last thing you're offered in death.

It's not that I felt I was outstaying my welcome. Invites to visit came thick and fast, but in village politics, there's a fine line between declining and accepting invitations. To accept one, is tantamount to accepting all, and the balancing act after three days of trying not to step on toes, was starting to wear a little thin.

It was late afternoon on the third day, that I decided on an evening crossing. I was sat down in Edwina Nash's kitchen, having yet another cup of tea. The bay was still veiled in a cheesecloth curtain of fog, but the forecasted breeze was starting to break it up. The afternoon forecast was calling for clear periods and light winds, ideal for an evening crossing.

"Any beer on the go boy?" I never thought I would be thankful to see three men on a drinking binge, but once again, I'm getting ahead of myself.

I left Branch at 6:30 pm, as the last whiskers of fog disappeared from the bay. The seas where calm, and a light tailbreeze helped me along. By 8:30 pm, I was nearly halfway across, but by 9:00 pm, was already in trouble. A strong southwesterly had picked up and was funneling down the bay; lop was forming under the setting sun, and sea-swells were rising into the dusk. By 10:00 pm, these same waves - topped in surf and seen through the gloom of a night sky - looked like fast approaching avalanches.

It wasn't the first time I'd attempted a bay-crossing at night. Normally, the wind dies as the sun sets. Navigation becomes easy, lights dot the coast and boat traffic is almost nonexistent. In fact, I prefer paddling at night, but this night, everything went terribly wrong.

By midnight, I'd made a pact with the devil. I was getting swamped by every third wave. I was wet, tired and very cold, but worst of all, my nerves were shattered. I still hadn't got a foothold on the far shore, and when St. Vincent's beacons of light disappeared behind its cape, I started to worry.

Conditions went from bad to worse, as I entered Holroyd Bay. I couldn't find the gut (small entrance) people had told me about to a sheltered pond. It was now after 1:00 am. I had been paddling for over six hours and my hands were raw and my eyes stung from sea spray. I approached the beach twice, but both times, the pounding surf and the telltale sound of water rushing over pebbles - denoting a steep beach - forced me back. I even had my headlamp on, but could not see how steep the beach was, or if it was guarded by rocks.

I could feel the beginnings of panic. It was now or never. I paddled again, as close to the beach as possible, but this time, I saw something; a house light. I took out my whistle and started blowing like crazy, then started to shout.

Minutes stretched into an eternity, then a door opened, a figure appeared, then a headlight, and within seconds, beams were racing towards the beach. I now knew that the worst that could happen, was if my kayak nose-dived through the surf and snapped its tip on the beach.

Trying to come ashore in breakers, is difficult at the best of times. Damaging one's kayak is one thing, being sucked under by a strong riptide and suffering a watery grave so close to shore, is another. The conditions bore all the signs of a strong undercurrent. I had heard of grown men being swept off their feet by rogue waves and drowning within spitting distance of land. These steep beaches generate strong undercurrents, like invisible rapids, close to shore, and they can carry a person great distances within only a few minutes. They can be deadly, are not always shown on sea charts, but are well-known by the people whose lives they border. That night, it was pitch black. I was wearing my life jacket and was prepared for the worst, so you can imagine my relief at seeing the cushion of friendly faces ready to catch me.

I think that my welcoming committee was more worried than I. They grabbed my kayak, even before it had come to a halt, then in three powerful heaves, bounced me up the beach's steep incline, onto level ground.

Ten minutes later, I stood steaming, next to a stove surrounded by my saviours. Up until that point, hardly a word had passed between us. They were clearly aware that they were dealing with a person who, at any moment, could tip over the edge. I was wound-up like a spinning top, shivering, not from the cold, but from the shear weight of my own insanity. I was in no mood for chit-chat, then Raymond Hawart offered me a beer. Within minutes, the dam burst. After the first sip of beer, I leant against their goodwill like a cut sapling, and was soon unloading my story as one does to a psychiatrist. They listened, joked, then laughed it off with stories of their own.

After sixty minutes, I was downright giddy. The night's events, at last, were dispatched. Even the thought that my kayak, still filled with gear, was exposed on the beach like a shipwrecked prize, ready for plunder, didn't bother me.

That night, I was billeted with Raymond's mother. It was past 3:00 am before my head hit the sack and within seconds, I was dead to the world.

The next morning, or was it afternoon? - I looked through the window, but my heart was for indoors. The bay was streaked with white flashing teeth. The waters were restless, paddleable, but ready to snap and gobble me up at the first mistake.

The decision to stay was made for me. Raymond, none the worse for last night's drinking, had other plans; I was now to become his project and he had already made up a calender of events. I was to go here and there, drink with his friends during the day and partake in the local shoreline rod and reel (albeit poaching) harvest of cod, but most of all, I was not to resist or question.

Raymond is a character. Built like a stick of chewing gum, with a skin with a surface that could have been molded in wax, he owned a motor-mouth. This man, in another life, could have been a facilitator for the rich and famous; a minder with a heart of gold. He wasn't the type of person to take no for an answer. His face would contort into a tragic mask against resistance, and would split and screech when I complied. Raymond was from the old school, from an era when men used their natural cunning to survive. He sought out my weak spots, like a wolf does with its prey, and I was soon putty in his hands.

I followed him around St. Vincent's like an obedient puppy for twelve hours, and it was during one of his planned pit-stops, that I met up with a group of Newfoundlanders with love in their hearts and revolution on their lips.

"What does tha mean, boy?"

Once again, liquor had loosened my tongue, and once again, I would pay the penalty. To fully understand this man's anger, not against me, but against the subject I'd uncorked, 'Make Work Programs', one has to fully understand the nature of that on the coast, and the people whose forces it moulded.

Seasonal work, before Confederation and the collapse of the fisheries, was more of a cottage industry than the government funded make-work programs of today. They had been instigated to bridge the gap between inshore to offshore, between outdoor to indoor, but had they accomplished what they started out to do?

I'd gone with the flow all day, and now I was to be rewarded. I'm a Luddite at heart. I love self-made men, those who are proud and independent, and now, I found myself surrounded by like-minded spirits.

"Like all things in life," this man said, "you don't get any-thing for nothing. I hate this make-work business. Over three generations of Newfoundlanders have lived under its cloud. They've fallen under its spell. They only made it up to keep the restless masses happy, to keep idle hands busy, and it's worked, Bernie. They've clear-cut our fish and left us the government twigs of make-work to live off. People have forgotten their roots, forgotten how their grandparents lived."

He went on to describe a life where men flowed from summer work on the sea to autumn woodchoppers on the land; a time when each village had a carpenter, a mechan-ic and a boat builder.

"We may have lived hand to mouth, but we were inde-pendent. In those days, people worked at their own pace, were surrounded by their families and didn't have to kneel before a boss. Sure, maybe the person who dreamed up the term, 'make-work program', had good intentions; thought we would all either starve to death or kill each other over the last cod or last stick of wood, but look at what's happened. On the surface, we've been civilized, doctored, educated, homogenized and tamed, but underneath, we are the land of the living dead."

God, I was in my element and they knew it, and no sooner did he finish, when another one of his friends picked up the torch and ran with it.

"I've worked on those programs, cut down bushes next ta' highway, built a fish plant that was never used, been re educated for jobs that never came, but I never depended on 'em, never planned around 'em, and never became their servant." Then, as if to underline his last comment, jocking-ly added, "rules were made to be broken," and pointed to the freshly gutted cod, readied for the frying pan. "Didn't you hook this one last night, Bernie?" he asked with a laugh. You could argue with his tactics, but not his logic. This, I told myself, is what I'd come to Newfoundland to see and hear, and that night, I wasn't disappointed.

True to his nocturnal habits, Raymond was still snoozing, as I paddled away the next morning. I left, not under darkening clouds, but with a heavy heart. I'd been given a royal send-off. A small group of well-wishers, some from last night and some who were just curious to see the man who was paddling around Newfoundland, pushed me off through a wave of enthusiasm. Without a doubt, that day was the low point of the trip. In all honesty, I didn't want to leave. I'd only just scratched the surface of newfound friends and craved to dig deeper. It's always the same for the traveler, here today, gone tomorrow; hello and goodbye. I know that I'm just a blip in their lives, a short story to be pulled out over the kitchen table. "I wonder what happened to that kayaker. Did he finish?" But still, after all these years, some partings hurt more than others.

By the time I was ready to leave, I was in tears, and no amount of swallowing could hold them back. I only left because I felt that I had to finish what I'd started and the idea of packing it in was worse, at that moment, than continuing. How I held it together and didn't fall apart in front of them is anyone's guess, but once I'd paddled out of earshot, I gave into my feelings and cried loudly.

I struck across the bay to Gull Island Point. A damp chill hung in the air and it was only a matter of time until the fog rolled in. It seemed to take all morning to paddle the bay. My rhythm was lost to sadness, and no sooner had I crossed to the far shore, when it too was lost, but this time to fog.

I was taking a time-out at the foot of some rocky outcrop, bobbing around in rolling swells, with my hand searching for the thermos between my feet, when I felt water.

There seemed to be a lot of water in the boat, so I checked my spray skirt. It was bone dry. Where was it coming from.....? Then, I remembered. I'd hit a sunker the night I paddled down Holroyd Bay. At the time, it only felt like a kiss; I hadn't even bothered checking it in St. Vincent's. Now, my imagination was running wild. I started to envision a gaping hole. Was I sinking? I reasoned that I couldn't have paddled so far this morning with a big hole; sure it had puddled, but I felt no flow.

I beached at the first opportunity and didn't have to look far to find the problem. The fiberglass repair job that had been done before leaving Corner Brook - a hair line fracture - was peeling away like dead skin from a bone. These fractures cause pressure leaks, invisible to the naked eye, but its weakness, if left unattended, would only widen, or God forbid, puncture on the next rock. To make matters worse, almost all the gelcoat on the underside of my kayak had been filed off.

I'm a rough and ready type of guy. Only twice, had I used driftwood to help pull my kayak up onto beaches. It had been dragged, bounced, and abused, down numerous pebble and rock-infested coves, and in the water, it had scraped and kissed more than one sunker. Now, I was paying the price. In places the fiberglass was so thin and translucent, I could almost see objects through it. The repair job that my kayak would require, would be large and complicated, and only in St. John's, could I make the repairs. I would need fresh water to clean the underside of the kayak and a dry place to patch it up with fibreglass. Luckily, there were no more bays to cross. I could follow the coastline like a tracer, and use the foam cushion that I sat on, as a sponge, if needed.

Two seals watched me paddle off into the fog. It was the last unbroken stretch of land I was to see until St. Shotts. Visibility was down to one hundred yards, and the sounds of occasional surf breaking on cliffs, kept me well away from the shore. I hate using my compass, but today there was no choice, and the only reason I risked it, was that there were no large bodies of water to cross. I had been told that this stretch of coastline was a minefield of sunkers. Forever watchful, at one point, when I was totally confused by the distinctive rushing sounds of surf breaking all around me, I stopped dead in my tracks. I was edging my way forward, not knowing if I was closing in, or paddling away from danger.

The fog only parted for a moment. In front, not five yards away, there was an unbroken line of table-top rocks. I immediately froze, in a whirlpool of motion. A silent breaker had sucked me back onto an exposed sunker. As I fell, its rounded top, weeping with surf, rose above my head. I was trapped, stuck to its side by the vacuumed space that the heaving swell had caused, and waiting for the inevitable onrush of water. All around, the sea seemed to bubble and boil, but when the swell returned, it neither crested nor surfed. It came from below and cradled my kayak as a protective mother would her child. I rose effortlessly into the swell, submitted to its forward momentum, and before I had time to react, it had carried me up and over the sunker, the line of rocks behind, and into the calm waters of a tidal lagoon. How I managed to stay upright or pass over the rocks, without even brushing my kayak, is beyond me. I had been taken completely by surprise, and not for the first time, found myself lucky to be dry, safe and intact.

Still not out of the woods, I was paddling in heavy fog, as well as a confused sea of clapping waves. I was closing in on Western Head at the entrance to St. Shotts. I'd heard that the tidal rips ahead, and especially the ones at the mouth of Trepassy Bay, that used its points at Cape Pine and Cape Race as sling shots of momentum, could be both strong and turbulent, so thank God for small mercies. The coastline, although festooned with hidden rocks, wasn't being pounded by surf, but still, it was frustrating.

I think it was the combined effects of the day's conditions: the penetrating, cold, damp atmosphere above, and the erratic behavior of the seas below, that stole my concentration. I'd not seen the sun all day, and was soaked to the skin, and was beginning to slap the water. My paddle strokes had shortened and lost their punch. Forcing myself to sit straight up in the seat, I focused motion on my shoulders and trunk, rather than my arms. I started reaching further forward into the water with my paddle, raised my elbow a little higher, readjusted my grip and started to rotate my upper body more. These changes didn't always work, and I treat them no differently than some people desert dance in hope of rain. It's hit and miss at the best of times, but this time, the difference was amazing. In no time at all, I'd regained my rhythm. My head cleared, blood started to flow, my eyes rediscovered the landscape around me, and the fog mysteriously lifted just in time to see a colony of puffins.

I was beginning to think I was born with a silver spoon in my mouth. In general, the weather had been brutal, but without a doubt, the hospitality had been fantastic.

I was spotted on arrival, this time at St. Shotts wharf, looking like a wet rag. The first thing Donna Hewitt asked me was, "Would you like to use my dryer?" One thing led to another, a cup of tea stretched into sandwiches, overlapped with an evening meal, was punctuated with videos and ended mummified in down covers.

Chapter: 10
Where have all the Lighthouses gone?

I left the next morning with my tanks full, smelling of roses, and with a snap in my stroke that I'd not had since leaving Corner Brook. I rounded the low-lying, reef-infested shoal waters en route to Cape Pine in a breeze. The morning was brilliant. The sun was out and its reflected rays were massaging my sore knuckles. Within the hour, I'd zipped open my wet suit, then bared myself to the waist. It was heating up quickly and although the conditions were ideal to cross Trepassey Bay from cape to cape, the impressive view of rusty coloured cliffs that tapered down its western peninsula to Baker Head, were just too good to pass up.

I was soon slicing through hundreds of ducks, while above, squadrons of gannets, white bellies flashing as they banked against the wind, flew in precision formations around me. All manner of ducks, disturbed by my presence, called out their displeasure, and everywhere, the sky was smudged by their wings. I slowly followed a contoured line of cliffs, exploring, taking time out to take pictures, and for once, I enjoyed being the tourist.

A bald eagle had captured a duckling. It flew with its soft prey dangling, swaying with each beat of its powerful wings, then an updraft took it away. An armada of minke whales glided by, so close that the smell of their breath was overpowering. Suddenly, a majestic humpback blew, not ten yards from my bow. Another, almost rising through the same wake, released a dusty jet, then melted away, sinking back in the same movement....awesome!

I was pointing my camera and shooting like a new-age big game hunter. I was spoiled with choice. The whole coastline was full to overflowing with the sight and sounds of wildlife, and I was soon searching for new film.

I started to let go of the land at Baker Head, but as I began traversing the bay, leaving the sheltered waters below its cliffs, a squall came from nowhere. I could have kicked myself. Paddling in shoal water, only four to six fathoms deep, waves were rafting and their windborne spit soon soaked me.

At Powlle's Head, the intermittent gusts were so overpowering that I took a pit-stop.

"How's it going me boy? You're the kayaking man I heard about." It was the lighthouse keeper.

I am sorry readers, but I'm from a different time; a time when community life was valued, and safety was more important than profit margins, so don't expect me to come down on the side of those who want to privatize lighthouses, to turn them into casinos, bed and breakfasts, or be converted into homes for people with too much money and too little sense. I had been on the water for over a month and other than hearing from Joe Drake, who mans the lighthouse at St. Jacques Island, I'd neither passed nor heard of any, until today, that were still manned. Where have all the lighthouses gone???? Good question.

I'm tired of turning corners, only to see some excuse for a lighthouse. These hightech replacements are gutless, shaped like oversized crystal balls on stilts, fully automated and are neither 'use nor ornament' to me. It is as if the old structures have been castrated and circumcised. If this is progress, you can keep it. The bottom line is, that all parties except the government, want to keep lighthouses staffed to help the marine community. They go together like wine and cheese. It's easy to see where priorities lie, when beams and forecasts are projected miles offshore. Automation is the new buzzword in the corridors of power, and to hell with the human costs in lost coastal jobs. Most accidents happen close to shore, not out to sea, and most deaths, within sight of land. Who understands coastal conditions more than the people who live on them? Who knows more about their quirks and quarks? These days, weather forecast are bland, full of coded messages, and may as well be radioed from Pluto.......but I digress.

The lighthouse at Cape Pine....now that's a lighthouse. It stands out from the cape like a huge erection and the one at Powell's Head, like the C.N. Tower in Toronto. They're not only landmarks for my eyes to rest on, when the weather seems to throw everything it has against me, and their fog horns, beacons of sound to guide me, but more importantly, knowing that they are manned, is enough to raise anyone's spirits.

Tom Corrigan, Powell's Head's lighthouse keeper, had spotted my yellow kayak from his kitchen window, met me on the beach, transported me back to the lighthouse on his ATV, then got his wife to feed me some freshly caught salmon. Tom is the last of a dying breed. He's closing in on retirement, so for him, the shifting sands of progress, bottom lines, profit margins and automation are in the future, but still, I detected a sadness in the man's eyes, when talking about these changes. Maybe he had seen too much; too many closures, storms and too much needless progress. Bound to the sea, like many of his friends and relatives, he'd seen the slow, cancerous progression away from inshore and the disintegration of a way of life. He told me that lighthouses were as important to outports as churches were to religious congregations. To him, they are not only symbols of a way of life, but living entities and homes of goodwill. He was certain that when he retired, there'd be no live-in replacement. Already, he was apprenticing a man from Treppassey, to take over his job when he retired; a maintenance man with a college degree, a man who would drive daily from his home, just to check and monitor a control panel. Someday, Tom's house would be converted into a helio pad, and all that would be left of Tom, would be his rhubarb patch, which anyone on the coast will tell you, is indestructible.

Before I left, he radioed ahead to the lighthouse keepers at Cape Race and the one at Greenspond, to keep an eye out for me. We parted on a promise. I promised him that I would try and find something poetic; something that would not only express his concern for the future of lighthouses on the coast, but that would express my love of them as well.....This is for you Tom:

When you've been caught out in a storm, it never leaves you. You never hear the wind after that, without remembering that banshee moan, the watery mountains, crests torn into foam.......but today, I was riding it out on land, sat by a glowing fire, high above the angry seas below, and the echoed cannon fire of waves hitting rock only made the lighthouse feel warmer.

Tom's hospitality led to a cat-nap. I fell asleep on his spongy couch and didn't wake-up until early evening. I could have stayed, but I don't like to leave with my plate empty. His invitation to camp on the cliffs and repair my boat was tempting, but I wanted to get to St. John's as fast as possible. I had mail to pick up, provisions to buy, and a new cockpit skirt awaited me. I was getting sick and tired of always being wet, especially my seat. In St. Shotts, I found a series of salt boils on my chest and two filled with puss on my bottom. It wasn't the first time, but I was still surprised. I'd had two showers in the last week, but maybe the two stretches of bad weather I'd passed through recently, leaving me continually wet and salty, were the cause. My wet suit was so salt encrusted in St. Shotts, that I swore that it could stand on its own legs, so before putting it in the dryer, I'd soaked and drained it twice. Using baby powder to dry myself, instead of a towel had become habit, but now, even that didn't seem to work. Antibiotic powder was needed and I knew that I could only buy this in St. John's, so it was just another reason to push on.

It didn't take long to paddle the distance to Portugal Cove. Once again, I had a dangerous cape to go around, and wanted to camp within shooting distance of it. I could have gone further, but the sun was low and there was a bite in the air. My tent erected on its wharf, I cooked, ate and fell asleep immediately.

Chit, where is the summer? I woke into fog, never a good sign, and when eventually the day came to life, my heart wasn't into paddling.

I'd also woken into a natural hangover. My head felt woozy and my nose ran like a leaky cup. Had I not been fogbound, I would have burned off their germs with a good healthy paddle, but I was trapped in a tent as wet and damp inside, as the fog-laden air outside.

I was royally pissed-off. It seemed that I'd spent more days storm or fogbound recently, than paddling. I knew that I was ahead of schedule. The plan was, six weeks to St. John's, then eight back to Corner Brook, but in one month, I'd only experienced a handful of sunny days, and waking up cold and damp is no fun.

That morning, I took a leak in the fish plant and got the shock of my life. It wasn't that my sex had shriveled. That's not unusual; it was my reflection in the washroom mirror. I'd aged twenty years in ten hours and looked like death warmed up. My eyes were bloodshot and had sunk into their sockets, my hair was knotted, my lips lined, and my wrinkled face looked like that of an old man. The skin on my hands was starting to crack and cuts oozed puss. My wrist had swollen and the slightest movement felt like sandpaper on glass, while my fingers looked like ripe sausages and my nails were as white as chalk. They were all symptoms of a person who had been submerged in water. I wasn't dying of cancer, hadn't caught flue or some sexually transmitted disease. No, Bernie was waterlogged.

Time is a great healer, and for me, it took only the time to walk from the wharf to the nearest variety store, to be cured. It's not that anyone could get lost looking for a variety store in Portugal Cove. It only has 1000 inhabitants, but in thick fog, looking for a store which could easily be in the basement of a house, was like looking for a needle in a haystack.

I never did make it to the store. Arnold Ward stopped me

in the road, invited me to meet his family, insisted that I drink a rum to put colour back into my cheeks, and that I stay for the night.........Saved by the bell!

The weather wasn't much better on the third day, but I pushed-off under the umbrella of a forecasted light breeze, and a promised late morning fog burn-off. For once, the forecast was right. The fog lifted its skirt as I rounded Cape Race, and Tom's promise of a lighthouse welcome materialized on cue. Three men appeared, waving like windmills from the clifftop. Cape Race is awesome, and its red and white lighthouse was icing on the cake. I didn't mind posing for pictures, even paddling through some dangerous surf between a point of land and some sea rock. The waves seemed mountainous, and I rose and fell like an air balloon, stuck on its surface. Green curlers were ever present, but few crested into surf. I was never in any danger, and if called back for an encore, would gladly have complied.

I had now turned the corner and was starting my slow reel-in to St. John's. After weeks of barren cliffs, sometimes topped with grazing sheep, it was a pleasant change to see trees, and after days of high waves, the water was flat again.

I made Burnt Point, as if paddling on a mirror, and it was just before I beached, that the sight I'd been waiting for, the one that National Geographic loves to cover, and one your average tourist can only dream about, began. I not only saw a group of humpback whales in an eating frenzy, but had a front row seat.

It was not so long ago, that hunting of whales and seals was an an essential ingredient of Newfoundland life. Their meat was a rich source of protein and their blubber, when turned into oil, an excellent pre-kerosene substitute for firelight. Times have changed; we are now living in an age of Greenpeace. Now, today's hunters are more likely to be armed with a camera and shoot through the eye of a lens, than your standard 303. Animal rights may be a dirty word on the coast, but their sympathizers are numerous and their access to the all-powerful southern media is a much easier sell for them than for your average Newfoundlander with a rifle. Personally, I came east to eat game, not to photograph it, but after today, I may change my mind. My first whale sighting came within a few days of leaving Corner Brook and now they had become an everyday part of my trip. They came in singles, pairs and in pods numbering as many as six. I spotted them 'rounding Capes on calm days, swimming against the currents down narrow tickles and, like today, between shoal and deep water, off the Avalon Peninsula. All these sightings had the same calling card - a noisy woosh - then silence. There are only a few documented cases of collisions at sea, but in my mind, one accident is one too many. Whale watching may be a safe passtime from a speed boat, but I can do without the unwanted adrenalin rush from watching within a kayak. Thank God, they are slow and predictable. Like a train trapped on lines, the only time they could hit you, is if you suffer from suicidal tendencies, or like today, pass over their food chain.

The first hint of today's treat came while paddling past Chance Cove. Dead caplin were everywhere. I found them washed up on rocks and marking the high tide on beaches. They were coming ashore to spawn and that meant a feast day for every seal and whale in the neighbourhood.

There is an old saying, "Man can't live on bread alone, and sex won't fill an empty stomach!" When I first arrived on the coast, I thought the fresh air and high sperm counts were the reason for large families, never thinking it could be their diet, until I started to eat fish. I have tasted smelt, trout, arctic char, salmon and rock cod, but caplin are in a league of their own. Deep-fried in flour, roasted or just plain dried, they are a meal in themselves, so who could blame me for taking time out to go sightseeing?

That afternoon, the sea was becalmed and there wasn't a hint of clouds in the sky. Underwater, rocks rushed up like mountains to meet me. On calm days, paddling shoal water is akin to low-level flying. Viewing sea life, through clear salt water, only magnifies its quality. Pebbles look like rocks and sea trout, like trophy salmon. For thirty minutes, I drifted through this scene, then suddenly, the curtain dropped. It was caplin, millions of them, a liquid pool of black on amber.

It didn't take long for the news to spread. A school of seals appeared, then a pod of whales. I couldn't have orchestrated the events better. I was right in the middle of the action and while seals swam towards me, whales circled just off the shore.

The seals struck first. One moment, a dozen heads bobbed up in front and the next, a thousand bubbles exploded underneath. Instant pandemonium, a flipper, blurred outlines and caplin shooting off in all directions. It was a case of survival of the fittest without table manners, an eating frenzy that passed within seconds. Moments later, the pod surfaced, then a lone seal, only feet from the kayak. It was an old square flipper. A large grey, with cat-like whiskers and puppy-dog eyes. I was on top of it immediately. Suddenly his whole body arched, snapped back like an elastic chord and crashed back under the surface. I'd been spotted and the noise set off a chain reaction. Moments later, caplin were jumping and the whole scene replayed itself, as seals rushed in for the kill.

It didn't end there. I was just turning for shore, when a thundering roar had me staring down a humpback. Who can be scared when a huge whale arcs out of the water, belly up? It was amazing. First one, then another humpback roared to the surface. Caplin were everywhere and those that escaped the jaws of the whales and seals, were eagerly awaited by scores of scavenging gulls lining the shore.

I was now almost halfway into my trip and today's experience was an added bonus. To an outsider like myself, sightings of game, whether it be a whale or sparrow, punctuated many a lonely day. I could count on the occasional osprey, where rivers emptied into the sea, and eagles had been a common sight on the southern shore. Large companies of drakes, gannets and even eider, were always following my progress. Terns could be counted on to drop by, following strong easterlies, and puffins were becoming a daily occurence. Then there was the day a lone mosquito hitched a lift, left momentarily, only to return with reinforcements.

The day ended quickly on a beach decorated with driftwood, with a brook of cool ice-water and a sheltered campsite. I lit a huge bonfire, smoked out the mosquitoes, then sat back into my appetite. Fire, water and shelter - a trilogy for a nomad; after six weeks, I wore its collective parts like a second skin. It had the brand of a rolling stone and would take more than a scrub down in St. John's, to wash off its ingrained rhythms.

Chapter: 11
Good Golly Miss Molly

Not again! Just as my body was adjusting to summer, autumn returned.

That morning, the only openings in the fog, came with the rain. It was that heavy, you could have mistaken it for a monsoon. The rain beat down so hard that it bubbled and spat like water droplets on boiling oil. It got everywhere. It forced its way through my waterproof poncho, streamed down my neck, pooled in my seat and stung my eyes. There was no escaping it.

After only five miles, I threw in the towel. I paddled into Renews with my tail between my legs, in search of shelter. Luckily for me, I wasn't the only one in a boat that morning. A friendly voice hailed me over, and I took refuge in his boat cabin below. Thoroughly wet, I stripped and changed, then hung over his oil-fired stove as if my life depended on it. The rain went on and on, and try as I might, clothed in every dry stitch of clothing I possessed, I couldn't warm up. It wasn't even 10 o'clock, yet continuing was the furthest thought from my mind, and so was camping. I couldn't envisage putting up a saturated tent, being confined to its damp, claustrophobic quarters this early in the day, so I decided to treat myself.

Sometimes it's good to close the door on travel, to become a private person again. I booked into Renew's one and only harbour-front bed and breakfast. It was one of those houses that wouldn't have looked out of place, had I paddled back in a time machine, to the days of sail. It could easily have been mistaken for an "Ann of Green Gables" scene. It was built in the days before pre-fabs and Wal-Marts, when house colours were primary, windows were single, not triple-pane, and where the only insulation was whatever you could spare to jam between walls. It may have been a little drafty, but it was cozy and fitted my mood perfectly. For once, it was pleasing to see a mackerel sky and to hear the drum-roll of rain, knowing I was inside. I showered, did my laundry, watched television and cat-napped the day away.

I spent the dying hours of the afternoon walking through slanting sunshine. It bathed the village in golden light and lit up the sea like the colour of autumn leaves. It seemed that the sun, or was it the rainbow that arced inland, had emptied houses onto the streets. Sunshine is sunshine, appreciated no matter where you live, but probably more so, in Newfoundland.

While walking back to the B&B, I gave into my hunger. An invitation came my way. I ran into the fisherman I'd met earlier in the day, and that night, was treated to a feast of cod soup and grilled salmon. Then, if that wasn't enough to stretch my belly, I polished off a plate of apple pie....Yeh, boy.

After today's paddle, I can understand why the southeast arm of the Avalon Peninsula could easily be seen as Newfoundland's answer to Disneyland's Waterworld. It has everything a tourist needs. Easily accessed by a coastal road with clifftop views and open sea horizons, it has, in Witless Bay, two island bird sanctuaries that are second to none. Home to thousands of terns, gannets and Newfoundland's national treasure, the puffin, it is a bird watcher's paradise, bar none.

From Witless Bay, the shoreline cliffs easily gave way to rolling hills, and her narrow inlets, to hidden outports. Everywhere, waterfront houses dotted the coastline like colourful checkers, and her icebergs, like frosted skyscrapers, floated by as if in a bowl of liquid turquoise.

I was continually buzzed by squadrons of low-flying ducks, and the noise was deafening, from the gulls on their cliff-top perches, and the colonies of puffins who nestled in burrows in the soft soil. Again, I saw humpbacks roaring out of the water and minke whales swimming by, like herds of watery elephants, nose to tail. The caplin were rolling on the beaches spawning, and everywhere I turned, there was either some bird, fish, seal, or whale chasing the bait.

That night, I pitched my tent down at the throat of Witless Bay. My camp was bordered on one side by the groaning sounds of a grounded iceberg and on the other, by a none-too-friendly goose with her brood. She'd been watching me from a safe distance, as I almost emptied a box of matches, trying to light a beach fire. I found few small pieces of driftwood, and what there was, seemed saturated. I could have used my stove, but lighting a fire and cooking on its embers, is one of the highlights of the day.

I love everything about fires; the beach-combing and the search for wood, its construction and trying to light it with one match. I love toasting my buns and watching the flames sparkle and spit into the night air. It becomes the centre-piece of my thoughts and if camped adjacent to it, an umbrella of protection. Cooking from one, is only a secondary concern.

That night, the twigs took forever to catch hold of a flame, and by the time I'd managed to brew-up a cup of tea, I must have burned enough dry grass to feed a herd of buffaloes. But that night, I wasn't the only one with thoughts of a fire.

Good Golly Miss Molly........ for a split second, Little Richard was back on stage, then a huge ball of light earthed me. It was after midnight, and I had woken into a party; not any party, but a July 1st extravaganza. What Newfoundlanders don't know about how to enjoy themselves, isn't worth writing home about, but I do draw the line on fireballs.

I was just too tired, too full of sleep to enjoy what they offered. They did come over to my tent, after their fire took hold, and offered me one of their beers and some pizza. I did try to relax into their presence, I truly did. I wasn't worried about my kayak, but about myself. It's one thing to let your guard down in someone else's home, and another, to do it miles from nowhere, surrounded by an hormonally unbalanced tribe of youth. I truly believe that the main reason I am given so much hospitality on the road, is because I leave stories, not babies, behind, and that the only thing a family man has to lock-up around me, is his fridge, not his daughter.

Ordinary parties are social games of sexual badminton, and this one was no different. After only one beer, the young girls seemed suddenly to be drenched in eroticism. There was a mood of rough excitement and all it seemed to need, was a match to ignite it.

She - the match, so to speak - arrived just after 1:00 am. You could feel it in the air.... testosterone. This young girl didn't so much wear her sweater, but had it painted on, and God knows what yogic exersize she knew, to be able to pull on her skintight jeans. She sashayed over to the fire, shot me a glance and instantly, my barometer hit red. The reptilian in me wanted to rape and pillage, and for ten minutes, it was touch and go. My body was saying one thing, but my brain was telling me to leave, so I left.

I woke-up for a few minutes, just before dawn, and from my vantage point above the lip of the beach, I could see them clearly. They sat with their feet towards their beach fire, like spokes on a wheel. They were talking in hushed tones and sometimes laughing. The whole scene radiated warmth. They were a good bunch of kids. Even though I'd not asked them, they had pulled my kayak further up the beach, away from the tide. I felt like going down to thank them and now wish I had, because when I woke into the sunrise an hour later, they were gone. The fire had sunken into its embers and they had retreated into their tents.

Evidence of their party peppered the beach 'round their fire, like discarded shell cases. A large crow was devouring a slice of pizza, while another picked away through a garbage bag of leftovers. Their mini-jukebox rested where I'd last seen it, atop of driftwood, and the empty six-packs of beer were neatly packed and ready for return.

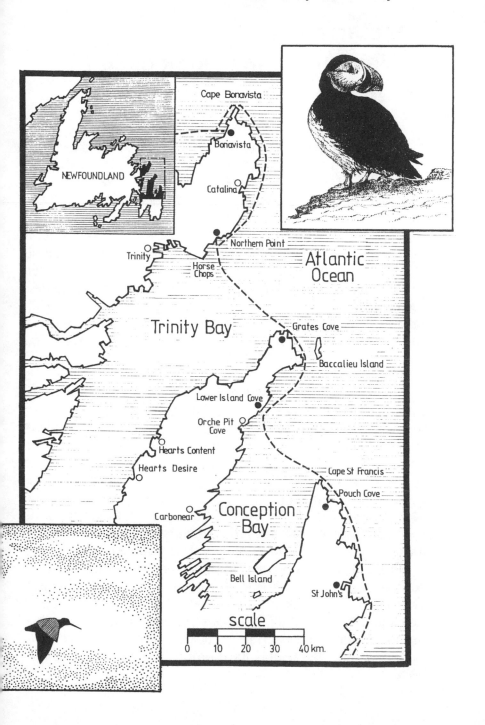

Cape Bonavista

Bonavista

NEWFOUNDLAND

Catalina

Northern Point

Trinity

Horse
Chops

Atlantic
Ocean

Trinity Bay

Grates Cove

Baccalieu Island

Lower Island Cove

Orche Pit
Cove

Hearts Content

Hearts Desire

Cape St Francis

Pouch Cove

Carbonear

Conception
Bay

Bell Island

St John's

scale

0   10   20   30   40 km.

Chapter: 12
A Diamond in the Rock called St. John's

The overwhelming thought in my head, the one that not only occupied the most space, but whose physical presence slopped round my ankles, was my leaky boat. I'd aggravated, no, angered my hairline fracture on entry that morning. The beach at Witless Bay had been steep, full of pebbles, yet too much like a kiddies' slide to ignore. I couldn't resist it, and with the help of two hungover, yet enthusiastic helpers - who pushed the kayak like a toboggan crew, - I was soon skimming over its pebbles, being launched from beach to sea. Brainless? Yes, but all the same, exhilarating. Now, I was paying the price, so it was with the overriding thought of repairs in mind, that I paddled around Cape Spear towards St. John's harbour.

Holy Chit!!!!! I was gob-smacked. In my mind St. John's harbour should be a world heritage sight. If Rangoon, Burma was once called the Pearl of the British Empire, then St. John's is the Diamond in the Rock of Canada. Reo de Janero has its world-famous, eleven-storey statue of Christ, spread-eagled above its harbour, and Manhattan has its impressive Liberty. I have seen Sydney's world-famous harbour front Opera House, and driven over San Francisco harbour's Golden Gate Bridge, but St. John's entrance, as seen through its natural, chiseled crack between vertical rock, called the Narrows, takes your breath away.

For me, its view is like a skirt rising in a breeze. That sudden glimpse of bare flesh above a gartered stocking. This flash from rock to harbour is infinitely more laced in mystique than the slow and more prolonged views the other harbours offer. The flash from rock to harbour, hits you like a slap on the face, and its memory lingers much longer because of it.

he twenty mile section from Shoal Point to Cape Anguille has the longest section of unbroken cliffs in Newfoundland.

Cape St. Mary's world famous 'gannet' bird sanctuary

Newfoundland and Labrador Tourism

Newfoundland's national treasure: the puffin nestle in burrow of soft soil above the cliffs

photo: Douglas Bisson

Occasionally low flying groups of puffins would breach the fo splinter in front of my face, then whizz past my ears in continu ous whines of noise

Newfoundland and Labrador Tourism
Notre Dame Bay
Majestic iceburgs float by as if in a bowl of liquid tourquoise

Newfoundland and Labrador Tourism
From the southern tip of the Avalon Peninsular to Notre Dame Bay, hardly a day past without spotting a humpback whale

Whoever coined the nick-name 'The Rock' for Newfoundland deserves a medal; it's beautiful, impressive and intimidating

Whitless Bay; Avalon Peninsular

Trumpet Cove: Bay of Islands

Looking north from Bluff Head towards the Lewis Hills;
Somedays the seas were glass calm, but those days were the
exception not the rule

Hermitage Bay; The Southern Shore
I paddled through a huge pod of playful porpoise that morning.
I gave up counting after thirty

When the sun comes out and the wind dies, there's no better
place to paddle around than the ROCK

Portland Creek; Northern Peninsular
Storm bound
The picture speaks for itself.....yuk!

Francois; The Southern Shore
Within a month the underside of my kayak had been scraped to
the bone - pebbled beaches can do that to you

Burgeo; Southern Shore
After a hair raising paddle that morning, I kissed the land,
thanked my mother for giving me the luck of the Irish, my
father for giving me the balls to try, and Newfoundland's liquo
control board for supplying the drink

Bonavista Bay
Newfoundland can be a bleak and hellish place, yet when the
sun comes out and the wind dies, and you find a sandy beach to
land on......it's heaven

top: McCallum: The Southern Shore
I have always been seduced by far away places; the ones cut off
by road, with rythms governed more by natural forces than by
the flick of a switch
bottom: Rose Blanche: The Southern Shore

Merasheen Island; Placentia Bay
The 'Mob's Batmobile' - have wheels will travel

Fishkot Island; Northern Peninsular
Echoes of bygone days

ewfoundland's Southern Shore is dotted with isolated beaches, none better than this horseshoe cove near Grand Bruit, behind Jaques Island

Exploits Island; Notre Dame Bay
After two months paddling it was nice to meet some fellow kayakers......but seven in one day!

Branch; St. Mary's Bay
After a month on the sea, it was time to do a spot of laundry

Agentia; Plancentia Bay
I find myself using the same wind that soaked me on the water
to dry my clothes on land. That day, I wasn't so much beaten-to
snot by the wind-born-surf as woterlogged by it.

A view from Cape Ray towards the Cabot Strait:
ɔmedays the seas looked like a lively snake-pit. After ten hours
in the saddle it wore me down like a soap stone

Port-aux-Basques
Two weeks into my trip and the strain was already showing. It
ʌas mid-June, yet the weather would get much worse before it
got better

The Outer Battery: St John's
Bruce Peter's home-away-from-home; a converted fishing stage
stuck like a limpit to rock

The Narrows: St John's Harbour

Cape Saint John

Encounters at sea were almost a daily accurance. Often these unplanned chats would lead to a night between clean sheets

Grates Cove: Trinity Bay

photo: Western Star, Cornerbrook
Home at last.....looking forward to one of Gino's Pizzas and some of Bob's home made wine

Paddling in the glacier fed Pacific water near Petersburg in Alaska!
........but that's another story

I entered St. John's through its narrows and once inside, the wind and waves belonged to another world. The harbour was breathless, but noisy, colourful, but tamed. At the moment of entry, a slot machine of questions was rotating in my head, and I didn't know which one was the most important; a roof over my head or one for my kayak. I was worried, really worried. It's one thing arriving with the sweat of travel in an outport, and another, paddling into the heart of a city. Cities, afterall, are busy and self-absorbed. I was feeling a little shell-shocked that day, not from the day's paddle, but from the tidal wave of sound and movement in front. The battering I'd taken, paddling through the confused seas rounding Cape Spear, had left me with little option than to beach at the first opportunity. My original plan had been to paddle further up the coast to St. John's dormitory community of Kitty Vitty, but the splashing of water between my feet, and my kayak's sluggish performance in waves, had changed my plans. Things couldn't have been any worse had I planned them that way, but it's at these moments, when life tests one's resourcefulness to the limit, that she also comes to my rescue.

Three Cherries.........! I hit the jackpot on my first try.

"My name's, Bruce Peters. Aren't you the lad who's kayaking around the island?"

How many times had that question come my way, but how sweet that day it was, to acknowledge it.

For the sake of underlining the obvious, I'm inserting my website's entry dated;

July 23rd
Hello and Goodbye

It's hard enough to say goodbye after one night with new friends, but after three, it's depressing. The upside to all this Newfoundland hospitality, is that the six weeks' supply of freeze-dried food, calculated to last until St. John's, has yet to be dented. In short, I have been spoiled rotten.

On the down side, it's hard to strike a rhythm. It is so

easy to turn over in bed and go back to sleep when you are between clean sheets. I have become lazy recently, spending more time stormbound than paddling and even some recovering from hangovers.

Am I feeling guilty? Not likely. One thing about getting older, is that not only do you accept your physical limitations, but enjoy the down-time, ten times better than in your youth. Let me take you through just a few of those relaxing moments:

I was not three days into my trip, when I was bedding down in a camper trailer, tucking into my first lobster supper with Art Hynes, in Port-au-Port. The next day, Gordon Gilbert gave me the keys to his cabin, near St. Teresa, and left me a supper of pickled rabbit. Then, there was the night I met "sunny" Russell Noseworthy, in Headlands, and went on a tear. The day I arrived, cold and wet in Port-aux-Basques, it was Russell Graham who not only came out to greet me, but provided the excuse to unwind with a bottle of rum. In Rose Blanche, Dennis Farrel lit the stove in his fishing stage, so that I could dry my equipment, then rolled out the red carpet. At Grey River, I stayed two days, stormbound with Stanley Young and his family, and in Point Rose, Philip Fazzel invited me in, out of the rain. In Point May, it was Peter Stacey who came to the rescue when I was dog-tired and wet, after rounding Dantzic Point. Richard and Cindy, in Lewis Cove, wined and dined me for two days, and Edwina and Donna in Branch, spoiled me rotten. Raymond Hawyart adopted me like a long-lost brother in St. Vincent's, and Sheila and Mary McGrath, in Patrick's Cove. Donna Hewitt braved a storm and the gossip, and invited me to spend the night with her family in St. Shotts, and it was Arnold Ward who insisted I spend the night with his family in Portugal Cove. Tonight, I have the keys to Bruce Peter's, home-away-from-home, below Signal Hill, in the small community of the Outer Battery, within spitting distance of downtown St. John's, and God knows where I will end up tomorrow.

The old saying, "It takes one to know one", doesn't only apply to travelers, but that day it was the only religion on show. Bruce, a sixties' child of peace and love - in a time when your thumb was the only passport you required, and your knapsack the only pillow you needed - was now a family man. He didn't travel anymore, but still kept his feet wet by opening his doors to shoe-string travelers and the occasional wannabe like myself.

As I paddled in, he was heading out on vacation. There was no time for the normal formalities that trust is based on, checking references or taking deposits in case of breakage. Like all travelers, Bruce relied on gut instinct - built up from years on the road - and it only took him the time required for my wet feet to grace his fishing stage, to make up his mind.

"Here's my keys," he said. "Sandy might pop in to do her laundry tomorrow. She can show you the ropes. Help yourself to what's in the fridge and my home brew is in the cooler."

We spoke for less than sixty minutes before he left, just enough time to exchange pleasantries and for me to explain the importance of finding someone to repair my kayak.

Not long after, I was standing under hot, wet needles, applying soap to my aching body. Even after only one day, I was a muddy hillside of sand, dirt and salt. I never stop marvelling at the ease of indoor living; the details, like hot water, drains, clean towels, carpets, bedsheets and food served on a table. It's a miraculous rebirth that occurs when I am warm, clean and able to wear clothes that are dry, floppy and loose. I could actually stand to smell myself and it felt good.

Bruce's home - a converted fishing stage, stuck like a limpet on rock, with the sounds of water lapping on pebbles directly under your feet - was without doubt, the prettiest thing I had ever stayed in this side of heaven. From his dining room balcony, you could almost reach out and touch the sides of vessels as they passed down the narrows, en route to the harbour. Situated on the waterfront, he had an unobstructed view of the city, and built almost entirely on vertical rock below a deadend road within a stone's throw from downtown, but away from its noises, it was almost totally isolated from the outside world. During the day, all manner of vessels came and went and at night, the city lit up like a Christmas tree.

On the first morning, I woke into a shadow. She was huge, probably seven stories high and as white, as white could be. From fifty yards out her bow almost filled the channel in the narrows. Passengers lined the decks, like chickens waiting to be fed; binoculars flashed in the sun, and the glint of video cams pointed and fired in my direction. She glided by, en route to her berth at the far end of the harbour, and her silent wake rippled along the narrows like a twisted serpent. I was awe-struck. She was a floating city, blotting out St. John's and plugging the harbour. I marveled at how she seemed to turn on a dime, and just as easily later that day, disgorge her passengers, as if one had kicked an ant hill. They got everywhere, clogging streets, swarming shops, and probably that evening, came as close as any government equalization payment scheme - with their ten hour purchase orgy of tourist nick-knacks - to paying off the Province's annual debt.

Later that morning, the Montreal container ship, Oceanic, steamed into port and seemed to plug-up whatever wharf space was left. I watched this coming and going most of the day, glued to Bruce's balcony, waiting anxiously for his friend to arrive and fix my kayak, but no sooner had we met, then I was pacing around St. John's, picking up my mail, my new cockpit skirt, and visiting the library to use their internet access to update my website.

That night, kayak fixed as good as new, with a new cockpit skirt to wear and weighed down in chocolate bars, I gave into Bruce's stock of home-brewed wine. Outside, I drank sundowners, with my feet up on the balcony and a cigar in my mouth. Influenced by alcohol, I allowed my mind to wander back into my youth; to the days when I was a receptive vessel, to be molded by parents and teachers alike.

I remembered the first time I saw images of Newfoundland. In those days Newfoundland was called the Dominion of Newfoundland, an off-shoot of the British Isles, not Canada, as it is known today. I was in a cinema, watching news reels of St. John's that showed its harbour, chocker-block full of fishing boats, of seeing clouds of seagulls fighting for scraps, and cod hung up on hooks that dwarfed the men who were weighing them. I remember seeing storm waves as high as mountains, ingrained in violent shades of white on black and the sight of outports, built under the shadows of monstrous cliffs with match-stick men, well-rounded women, and hordes of children playing around boats. My memory held pictures of a majestic schooner under sail, being swallowed up in fog, and icebergs the size of office towers and whales, chased on the high seas for their blubber; but always, there was news of some watery death. It looked like a bleak place, full of extremes. Not exactly a hospitable land for a nipper like myself, but these images had beckoned to the adventurer in me, and planted the germ that fifteen years later, would flower into immigration. It wasn't so much those images, as powerful an influence as they were, that lit the fire of adventure in my belly, but one man, a school geography teacher, whose gift of animated story telling was more suited for the stage than the classroom. His name was Mr. Dooley.

Mr. Dooley, or Old Tom as he was fondly called, was an Irish Catholic who could trace his family tree back to the potato famine and the forced labour of captains who press-ganged workers onto boats to sail to the New World. I remember Old Tom having legs like stilts, hands that could block out the sun, and a smile that could light up the dullest of lessons. He built our forty-five minute lessons around his trips, and spread germs of travel like confetti in the wind. His words were like seed pods with wings. They flew straight out of his mouth and into our youthful heads. He would talk about his trips to Egypt and India, of seeing the Pyramids and the Taj Mahal. He'd visited many continents, experienced many civilizations, but one in my mind, stood head and shoulders above the rest, Canada. I remember his talks about his trans-Canada railway trip, northern Ontario's endless forests, inland lakes bigger than oceans, and polar bears, moose, eagles and wolves. He would pass around pictures that he'd taken of snow-capped mountains, endless prairie horizons and waterfalls too big for youthful imaginations to comprehend. But one place above all else captured my imagination, the Jewel of the Commonwealth as he called it, the British protectorate, known as New..found..land, as he would pronounce it. It was this island, with its romantic place names, rugged cliffs and end-less coastline, that caught my imagination the most. Maybe it was because I, too, was born on an island, spent endless lazy summer days by the sea. I'm someone whose ears, even to this day, yearn for the call of seagulls, whose nose loves the smell of rotting seaweed and who's eyes forever search for the sea's hypnotic rhythms. Maybe it's the sum total of those ingredients that drew me to Newfoundland, and in particular, to kayak its coastline. For whatever reason, sitting down that night, listening to the harbour fog horn herald in a bank of mist, it felt right to be there; the perfect enviroment for a sea-loving boy's memories.

Even though my salt boils had disappeared and the cuts and bruises on my hands and knees were healing rapidly, I decided to stay one more day. Last night, I had abused my body, drank too much, and almost emptied two bottles of Bruce's, home-made wine. Not in a fit state to leave, I had woken into a mega hangover. On rising, my head had sunk into my chest, my belly into my bowels and my legs could only crawl. Before my brain even knew I was alive, I was on my knees in front of the toilet. I was retching, suffering, full of self-hatred. The radio sounded like a wasp in a jar, and when I made the fatal mistake of flushing the toilet, a thousand sledge hammers beat my head to pulp. Even a morning cereal didn't take purchase and it was almost noon before my head cleared.

That day, the sun seemed to hover directly above the harbour, like a golden disc. My body craved it. I alternated my time between deck and kitchen, feeding on rays and fruit in equal doses. It felt great not to wrestle with the daily demons of travel. I know that I am not going to win a lottery, garner the Booker Prize for literature, or uncover some hidden treasure during my trip. I'm comfortable with the knowledge that I'm not a born winner, but I'm also determined not to fail.

I was at the halfway stage. The worst of the weather was behind me and I could now expect more good days than bad. There were only two more hurdles to cross; two seas within a sea. They had been the main reasons that I had decided to go against conventional wisdom and coastal currents, and paddle Newfoundland anti-clockwise. They were both known for generating strong currents and winds, and they were both - so my Coastal Pilot Manual advised -

to be crossed under caution. Their names were, Trinity Bay and Conception Bay, and the term, under caution, meant seeking out local knowledge.

The phrase 'Local Knowledge' appears frequently in government literature, but also in discussions of sea navigation. It is a term rarely used on land with as much authority as it is at sea. I use this knowledge all the time, and even though I carry a complete set of topographical 1:250,000 maps of Newfoundland, used as a daily reference, have sea charts that cover every inch of its coastal waters, and have the seaman's bible, the Marine Weather Guide, at my finger tips, I still give local knowledge veto rights over everything.

All these aforementioned references, whether charted, mapped, written or calculated, are not set in stone. Channels open and close as sands shift and tides surge with the moon and sun's angle influences wind velocities. You have to be a rocket scientist to pour all those into your head and come up with an answer, and that's why local knowledge is so important.

Points of land can generate their own localized conditions and so can seas within a sea, and both of these bays, with jaw spans in excess of twenty five miles, are oceans of tidal water unto themselves. I wasn't exactly looking forward to crossing them, but at least the two things I'd planned for - weather and health - were now tilted in my favour.

When the sky is blue, the sea calm, and visibility unlimited, it can make your spirits soar. It was one of those days when the sea seems to embrace you and icebergs wink and glitter in the sun. The rest in St. John's had done me a world of good. It felt great to be on the water again, feel the crisp sea air on my skin and grip and punch the paddles through water again. I fell into a rhythm early and before realizing it, had paddled over fifteen miles, well on course to make Cape St. Francis before late afternoon.

I was taking a break at Black Head, nestled inbetween

two rocks, stretched out in my kayak, and enjoying the view of the cape's lighthouse ahead. While I sat there smoking a cigarette, a raindrop fell on my head, then another, then another. I looked up to see a turmoil of grey clouds, moving out to sea. Within seconds, the sky was black and the rain was in sudden free-fall, and not for the first time, my tail dropped, as the wind and rain rose in force.

I made Pouch Cove as the clouds were clearing, put up my tent under sun, then cooked and shared my meal with every mosquito within hailing distance.

The early evening sun turned my tent into a sauna, heat radiated inwards, and outside sounding like an out-of-tune chainsaw, a thousand mosquitoes hovered around my tent waiting for their supper, but I didn't care. Summer had finally arrived.

That night, the sun set softly through billowing clouds. Warm colours washed over the hills and sea, and the Avalon lifted its veil to smile. A sweet smell of hashish was in the air and mellow music came from below. I wasn't totally alone. Camped within a stone's throw from Pouch Cove's steep slip-way, I was sleeping on common ground.

Some things never change. It was a group of youngsters acting out the timeless rights of passage. Cities may have their shopping malls and parks, but here on the coast, their meeting places are as varied as the colours of a rainbow. Each community has its magnet; a place that draws both young and old alike to its core. Sometimes it's an unused fishing stage and sometimes, a government wharf. It could be a shed or a garage with a view, a deserted beach, or like tonight, under the eaves of a fishplant.

I did think twice about joining the group, but a good night's sleep seemed more important. Tomorrow's bay crossing, would be both a physical and mental challenge. I'd be paddling in unchartered waters, and at that moment, wanted to be alone with my thoughts.

Chapter: 13
Seas within a Sea

When certain wheels have been set in motion and cer-tain cogs have meshed, you get caught up in its momen-tum, and when that happens,there's no turning back..!

I set off late from Pouch Cove. It had rained hard in the morning. I'd popped my head out, seen a seagull scream past, and was just slipping back into my sleeping bag, with every intention of writing the day's paddle off, when the cou-ple who's garden I was camping next to, invited me in for breakfast. All the signs - angry clouds and howling winds - were telling me to stay put, but it's strange how a platefull of bacon and eggs can affect one's judgement.

It's easy for a vegetarian to blame pork for upsetting one's bio-rhythms, but I'm not a vegetarian. It's just that a full stomach gives me false courage, and that's why I crossed Conception Bay in a storm.

The Bay's crossing started well enough, and even when the funneling winds and strong shoreline currents that Bell Island in known to influence, picked up within minutes of leaving Cape St. Francis, I was ready for them. In fact at the halfway point, I was so relaxed into my rhythm, so confident that I would cross without incident, I got out of the cockpit to stretch my legs over the sides to take a break. I even noted in my diary that night, that I was actually laughing at my pre-trip nightmares of open water. I was, after all, as fit as a fiddle, and the late afternoon sky was cloudless, but just because there is no movement above, doesn't mean there isn't any below. The tide was full in, there was only a hint of a swell, and the only breeze I felt, came from the sea, but then the tide turned.

Within minutes, waves started to raft, peak, then lob over. I was now getting continually broadsided, pushed out down the bay and away from my planned landing. What should have been a fifteen mile crossing, was already past twenty and still climbing. My plan to land at Western Bay Head, flew out of the window with the wind. It was blowing so strong, close to shore, that try as I might, I just couldn't puncture a way through. It must have been blowing at gale force, cornering around points of land and picking up momentum as it headed towards open sea. First, the sheltered waters at Ochre Pit Cove slipped out of my grasp, then Northern Bay passed at a gallop. The wind was now acting with the tide, and every so often a rogue wave would completely swamp me.

At Burnt Point, I was at my wit's end. At the best of times, I hate having to surf, especially when the waves are steep, but I had no option. For one hour, I had purposely drifted with the wind and waves, hoping that the conditions would change, but I was rapidly approaching Flamboro Head. It would be now or never. I knew that once past its point, the land slips away into the dangerous, open waters around Bay de Verde. The shoreline was less than a mile away, and although I was facing it, couldn't make any headway.

I turned with the waves and the wind just past Job's Cove, and immediately fish-tailed, nearly capsizing. It was like driving over black ice; the only thing you can count on, is your forward momentum. I like a storm and being tested, but this was more than enough. The crossing had worn me down, not physically, but mentally. Conception Bay had played a cat and mouse game with me for over seven hours. Now, within a stone's throw from shore, the waves were so steep that they were passing under me like lines of fast moving soldiers. I was just bracing and steering. It took all that I had, to stay upright. Every now and then, I turned and steered for the shore, dug in and paddled like hell, then found myself having to back-paddle away from sunkers. By now, the left side of my face was chapped, my left hand dead to the world, and the left side of my lower back felt like a red-hot poker. I was telling anyone that could hear me, that if I got out in one piece, I would lead a good life. I would start going to church again, stop smoking, and never let dirty dishes stand, just to get me out of here!

I lied of course. No sooner had I stepped on land, when I lit a cigarette. So much for the repentant sinner. Well, I did kiss the ground.

Lower Island Cove's wharf threw me a lifeline in the form of a small concrete arm of stone, a water breaker. I'd approached it in overdrive, hooked its back eddie and pulled myself up to its slip-way. Thank God for small mercies.

Nothing worth having, comes easily in this life, and I truly believe that over the years, I've paid for my luck. Once again, my weather-beaten face not only opened the door to people's hearts and their larder's, but this time, to a phone call, and the roof of hospitality that evening, led me to the Gillingham Family, in Ochre Pit Cove.

I'd cast the dice that morning, not knowing how they'd land. More often than not, they fall between the cracks of life, but today, as on so many occasions on the Rock, they turned up trumps; three square meals, a shower and a night between clean sheets. What else can a traveler ask for?

The following morning, Roger Gillingham drove me from his home, back to where I had left my unattended kayak. I'd neither tried to hide it, secure it to the wharf, nor empty it. I was beginning to think of myself as blessed, like I had some Dark Angel - hopefully a warm-hearted Hells Angel hit man - looking after me. I like to think that whoever is out there, hovering over my shoulder, listening to my curses, is big, owns and drives a stretch limousine, and a Harley Davidson, is tattooed from head to foot, and has a beautiful sexy lady waiting for me in case it's my time.

Everything about that day was larger than life. Baccalieu Tickle lived up to its reputation for confused seas - it's here that ocean currents rise almost vertically from 40 to 10 fathoms, - and its cornering winds were horrendous. The tickle's entrance looked like the gates of hell, and its seas were not only confused, but rafting against a falling tide. In these conditions, a rudder is useless. The surf gripped me like a vice, forced me forward, as if in a rapid, and slapped me around like a schoolyard bully. I was flying, spending more time stroking fresh air than water, and being carried more on top of surf than in it. I was going up and down like a yoyo, facing cliffs one second and open sea the next. Locally, they don't call the waves of confused seas, clapping waves, for no reason. They hit you with chest-high walls of water and come at you from all directions. Another time and place, I could have enjoyed it, but not today. Yesterday's experience had taken more out of me than I dared to admit. Passing through this turbulent sea, felt like an eternity. It kicked and bucked for thirty minutes, then as suddenly as it started, it stopped.

At Goldmine Head, my fortunes changed. It was like paddling towards the end of the world. In front, Trinity Bay, yawned out into a distant haze. It was a wild spot to stop, not a place to be caught out in a storm, but the view was spectacular. It's on the lip of an abyss. I literally felt giddy, like a tight-rope walker that looks down and gets vertigo. There were no human signs to latch onto, no ship, boat, plane, animal, bird, no bobbing trap markers. It was as though I stood alone on the planet. The immensity of the sky roared at me. My tank gauge went from near empty to full, in less than a minute. What a sight! I wrestled with the idea of cutting straight across the bay. A thirty mile crossing through night seemed, at that moment, like a walk in the park. In the last hour, the wind had died completely. The sea was flat and inviting and I'd even started to angle across. I was about a mile out and in a world of my own, when a whale surfaced and burst my bubble. Sixty minutes later, I was greeting yet another invitation, this time in Grates Cove.

"How, she going boy?"

What makes big men shy and small men aggressive? Who cares? Carl Martin looked like a ruffled pillow and just as cuddly. Ex-RCMP, with the gate of a giant, gravelly voice of a six-pack-a-day man and a handshake you wouldn't want to argue with, opened his heart and let me in, as if I was his long-lost brother.

We met, as often is the case with the best things in life, by chance. I'd been offered a workshed behind someone's house, to bed-down in and was waiting out bad weather, biding my time for the right moment to cross Trinity Bay. I'd just popped down to the harbour to check the day's marine weather forecast, and was walking back up the hill, when a pick-up truck stopped. The rest is history.

Carl and I were a match made in heaven. The tall, sub-dued volcano with the cross of seriousness that all large men seem to carry, and moi, short, fiery and the self-appointed opinionator of the universe. From the word go, Bernie was a happy camper. I slipped into step with Carl's easy rhythm like an old glove, and in Vicky, his wife, I met a lady who's passion for life held no boundaries; the Dynamic Duo, as I called them, the free-spirited artist and the disciple of discipline. They fed off each other in the only way opposites can, and for two days, I lived in their reflec-tive glow. They wined and dined me, handed me the remote control and allowed me to vegetate in front of their televi-sion. In two days, I must have watched over a dozen videos, told as many true stories as lies, and covered a mul-titude of subjects, varying from politics, the fish moratorium, to the best ways of growing vegetables. We must have set the world to right scores of times. I reveled in the cut and parry of regular life, and within their four walls of normality, I was totally at peace. That I could stay longer than two nights, was never in question. How I could leave without staining my cheeks, was another. Hello and Goodbye, Hasta La Vista; the stronger the root, the deeper the cut.

"The grass is always greener", so the saying goes,"on the other side." I've always been a misplaced traveler with cravings for stability, and Carl turned into my alter ego. For two days, he shared his home with me and was the calm in the eye of the hurricane; the dreamer who sits back, lost in the crowd, but always noticed. Too many sentences have been written and too many images sold in the pursuit of adventure, when the greatest adventure is family life itself. I can't speak for women, but I know that many men envy my lifestyle. The universal free-wheeler; a girl in every port. If only they knew. A root transplanted, can be stumped at birth. Stability, constant care and food are their staple diets. I am just a side-show; a story teller for the masses; a root in constant motion. "But for the Grace of God, go I." For two days, I lived the life of normality, just one of the boys; just another Joe who could pick his nose with the best of them, fart up a storm after a plateful of beans, but most of all, just be himself. This experience, this injection of normality, hadn't been the first on my trip and no doubt, wouldn't be my last, but when I eventually left to cross the bay, I knew it had been special. A male bonding, par excellence, and something I knew would pass the test of time.

That morning, I tried the impossible. I had a printout of the marine tide tables, and just heard on the radio, the day's wind directions and velocities. I was juggling them around in my head, weighing out the options. Trinity Bay's western shoreline lay hidden behind fog, but the bay was still. I was trying to make up my mind whether to cross the bay from Grates Point to a peninsula of land, locally known as the Horse Chops, or paddle down the bay to New Melbourne and cross over to Deep Harbour. It was six of one and half a dozen of the other. The 5:30 am marine weather forecast had called for light to moderate winds and for the fog to clear. I could paddle down to New Melbourne and enjoy the coastal cliffs, then scoot across the fifteen miles of open bay, or go twenty miles, point to point to Horse Chops, and rely on my compass. I wasn't bothered about the extra mileage or even the fog; it was just those damn currents that local knowledge had warned me about. I had been told that the waters at the bay's mouth could be especially dangerous if an off-shore wind picked up. It was a place where outgoing tidal currents meet incoming Atlantic swells. Those colliding forces, even under moderate conditions, could stack up waves like ruffled feathers. I could have sat down with a calculator and worked out the tide tables, left near low tide and hoped that the funneling effect of midafternoon down-drafts would start when I was already ashore; but I'd tried all that before, and no matter how intelligent I thought I was, or how prepared on paper I became, Newfoundland's weather had always second guessed me.

As Carl said, "The weather waits for no one", and by 6:30 am, I was in the water with my bow pointed towards what I hoped was Horse Chops, on a bearing of north by northwest. My decision to go point to point that morning, was the best I'd made on the trip. The coastal fog burned away on cue and the bay's sea, except for two turbulent channels of strong counter currents, was calm. If anything, it was a piece of cake. Even when the cornering winds around Horse Chops forced me to change my landing spot, I couldn't have asked for a better place to beach.

It had only taken five hours to cross the bay. I was not only brimming with confidence, but bursting with energy. I was speeding towards an arm of rock called Northern Point, and was being pushed along by cornering winds. The seas were confused at its elbow, but invigorating. In front, was a small steep, beach of pebbles; sunkers were left and right of me and steep forming breakers guarded the beach. Navigation in a kayak is always a little tricky in these conditions. Under normal circumstances, I would have given Northern Cove a miss and would have continued, but the views of it were amazing.

Bordered on one side by a five hundred foot face of rock and on the other, by lush forest, it was a veritable zoo of wildlife. I saw a moose grazing in a gut, eagles flew in spirals above, and seals' heads were popping up and down like a wolf pack of submarines. Almost every ledge of rock was white with gulls, and whales seemed to be surfacing everywhere. Surely, I thought, the caplin will roll tonight?

I was approaching an entrance, probably only twenty yards wide, and was heading straight between two rocks. While judging the waves and waiting to sprint into a forming crest, a rogue wave rose and crested behind. It carried my kayak at incredible speed. I shot past the angry teeth of rocks that guarded the beach, up and over an exposed sunker with a smile that could have snapped me in two, and was halfway up the beach's 45 degree incline before I had time to react. If ever there was an occasion to have an audience and take a bow, that was it, but there was no way I would have gone back to take an encore...... once was enough.

Now this is the life! I have always loved storms when viewed from the land, especially those weathered, like today, from within a derelict cabin, when gusts make old joists creek and groan and the pellets of rain that strike a window, are just reminders of one's good fortune.

I could have left the cabin that morning, but was glad that I stayed an extra day. Yesterday, during my approach to Northern Cove, my eyes had been too preoccupied with spotting wildlife to see the cabin. I only noticed it after erecting my tent and only found its door open by chance. Inside, I had spotted a guestbook, and notes of thanks from duck hunters were pinned everywhere. It never ceases to amaze me, how trusting people are on the coast. This attitude of, leave as you find, was a simple rule. A cabin door unlocked, is rooted in common sense and built on the knowledge that next time, it could be your turn to be caught out in a storm.

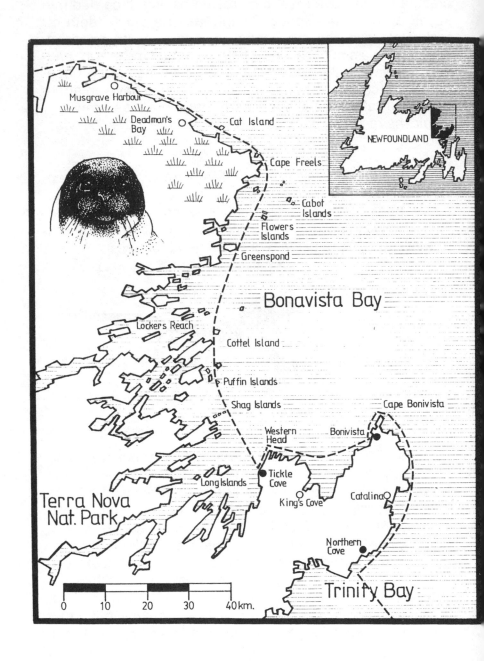

Musgrave Harbour

Deadman's Bay

Cat Island

Cape Freels

Cabot Islands

Flowers Islands

Greenspond

NEWFOUNDLAND

Bonavista Bay

Lockers Reach

Cottel Island

Puffin Islands

Shag Islands

Cape Bonivista

Western Head

Bonivista

Terra Nova Nat. Park

Long Islands

Tickle Cove

King's Cove

Catalina

Northern Cove

Trinity Bay

0   10   20   30   40 km.

Chapter: 14
Sea of Haze

I woke into fog and a pebbled beach, ankle deep in spongy spawn. Dead caplin littered the ground at my feet, and feathers stained the milky, grey sea that I was to paddle. The gulls were still there, but fewer in number. I could just make out two seals resting on a rock and the noise of a lone whale crying through the mist. I judged the fog to be localized. It was damp, but not cold, and there were hints of shadow at ground level and pigments of blue in the sky. I set off that morning with few goals. The route to Melrose was simple, sea to the right and land to the left.

It turned into a liquid morning. The sky and sea fused as one, and although there was a light wind, the fog stole all depth from the sky. The sun, shattered into a thousand fragments, could still be plotted, but at ground zero, there was little for my eyes to latch onto. I was going at a slow, pace but enjoying the ride because the views below the mist were enchanting. Sunkers and ragged edges of rock materialized like hallucinations, and the air was alive with the muffled cries of nesting birds. Ducks were everywhere, but invisible and nervously chattering. Occasionally low-flying groups of puffins would breach the fog, splinter in front of my face, then whizz past my ears in continuous whines of noise. A whale breached, and I was almost on top of it before it submerged. At one point, a strong downdraft tore a patch of fog apart and light charged down, turning the sea into a lagoon of blue neon, but generally speaking, the morning views were at a premium.

I followed the groaning sounds of a harbour buoy, but no sooner had I passed it, when the fog lifted above the cliffs. The tapered views ahead now rose and opened like flowers under the sun; lush, green vegetation gave way to bald rock, and empty skies, to squadrons of puffins.

A receding tide, was carrying me and miles were ticking

by. I was hugging the coast and enjoying every minute of it, stripped to the waist as the sun beat down.

I was approaching Maberly Provincial Park, marked on my calender of places not to be missed. I had been fully prepared to camp out in a week's worth of bad weather, so as not to miss out on its views. The section between Catalina and Cape Bonavista is home to colonies of puffins, gulls and gannets, and its rugged, cathedral-shaped coastline is world-renowned. I was on the crest of the wave; not only was the weather smiling at me, but the seas were as flat as a board. Then a yellow zodiac filled with camera-ready tourists punctured my mood.

Chit! I was so pissed-off, I could have screamed. It's easy to go back now and reflect on my anger, but it's harder to justify it. Just because I'd spent six man-powered weeks padding there, had stubble on my chin, and was bathed in sweat, didn't give me any more rights than those who showered daily and drive SUV's. It is, of course, hypocritical of me, to rail against tourists when I, too was one myself, but nonetheless, I couldn't escape the fact that mass tourism could ruin the very things that people want to celebrate.

All in all, I had a great day. The soily cliffs above Elliston were alive with burrowed puffins. Brilliant white gulls stained ledges like snow flakes and dark feathered ducks nestled in sea water like droplets of spilled ink. The rocks and cliffs around Cape L'Argent rose out of the seas like splintered ramparts, some as pointed as needles and some as squared as highrises. Caves begged for more than a second glance. An iceberg, shaped like a pirate galleon, and surrounded by melting bergy bits, crackled and popped under the late afternoon sun, and everywhere, whales were breaching. The highlight of the day came when one humpback glided only feet under my kayak....wicked! It looked huge. He'd been following my progress for over one hour, sometimes rising and sometimes rolling over to one side, before cracking his dorsal fin into the sea.

I rounded the intimidating rock face of Cape Bonavista

just as the first signs of colour were filling the sky. A damp breeze was picking up, and the menacing formation of clouds coming out of the west, soon took away tomorrow's views in veils of rain.

As the sun set, I beached just before the town of Bonavista. I ignited a fire of driftwood and was cooking in overdrive as the rain started. It peppered the beach and darkened the rocks in seconds, and right after I'd retreated to my tent to eat, the heavens opened and it began to pour down.

That night, the rain drummed the tent incessantly; same tune, same rhythm. Sheltered from the wind by rock, it only had one direction, but that was the only good thing that came from my camp's location. It soon started to pool and puddle from below. I had bought some waterproof spray in St. John's thinking that it would be a cure for another Harbour Breton kind of experience, but it turned out that I'd wasted my money. The water was coming from yet another a tear....!

BAAAAAAAAAAAA...............
BAAAAAAAAAAAA...............
BAAAAAAAAAAAA...............

Bloody fog....I shouldn't really complain. I'd been told, on numerous occasions, that Newfoundland manufactures the stuff for export. I'd even heared that it was their provincial gift to the rest of Canada, their share of the Federal Government Equalization Program. Well, I had plenty of time that morning, to mull over this thought. I'd woken at 6:00 am, rolled over, then cat-napped till 9:00 am. The rain had woken me - always a good sign of fog break-up. King's Cove's beacon of light was barely visible across Blackhead Bay. I took a bearing of west by northwest and pushed-off, but no sooner had I let go of land, when the rain stopped, the wind died, and the fog banks rolled back. It was pathetic. For thirty minutes, I played with the idea of crossing the bay, testing its waters and my ability to hear in the fog, hopping from one patch of clarity to the next, then back again.

I would nuzzle forward, check my compass, then scurry back within sight of shore.

Past the five hundred yard mark, the world stopped; panic plus claustrophobia, my achilles heel, struck and my tail dropped. On my second attempt, I may have paddled out one thousand yards, but when I heard the pulsating engines of a ghostly dragger, I lost it. What a wimp....!

The bay was less than ten miles across, point to point, shallow, known for even tides and nothing really to worry about. If only I could trust my compass. Once you're in this kind of cycle, the one that doesn't want you to travel blind, it's hard to break loose. I was beginning to think it was all Bernie deserved. The great, macho voyageur, unshrinking in storms, but throw fog his way, and he cries foul. The problem is, the worse it gets, the more it seems true. I was beginning to think I had it coming to me, as if the weather only came in two colours; black, or the red heat of passion. Before I started, I knew that I would see a lot of fog. My friend, Denis Jean, in Sept-Iles, had offered me his GPS, even offered to teach me how to use it, but I'd declined; maybe it's my age, or maybe it's some genetic mental block against modern technology. Whatever, I knew they were only excuses. I'm just too stubborn to change, full stop.

Finally, more out of embarrassment than courage, I paddled into the unknown. For three hours, I was lost to the world. Occasionally, the fog would rise and I'd see a distant flash of surf on rock, but more often than not, I was cocooned in mist. By early afternoon, I was closing in on the only point of land that I could see, Southern Head, which would become the first of five amazing fingers of land; five great big pillars of rock - dark, damp and lifeless.

All morning, I had noticed the seas climbing. There'd been a storm out in the Atlantic a few days earlier, so I wasn't surprised to find a sea on, around Western Head. I was still over five hundred yards away from it, yet I could hear the dull thud of waves slapping on rock. Monstrous sea swells were rolling out of the mist and kissing their reflective twins in sprays of surf.

I took a detour. I had to. The seas at the base of the Head looked like a churning lake of aerated cream. A salt mist stung my eyes and the flotsam of surf collected in a current line of soap bubbles. I stayed there, one hundred yards from the head, rising and falling in the swells and enjoying the flash of surf on rock and its delayed report. It was there, bobbing up and down on the circumference of the action, with a mug of coffee in my hand, that a speed-boat punctured the fog down Tickle Cove, stopped its motor and glided towards me.

"Fine day, boy. Fog some t'ick, eh?"

By now, these words held little currency. I half expected someone to say, "super fine day," when the sun came out, but words aren't the only constants that men use at sea to comment or to judge a persons character.

"Have you a light, mate?" I asked them. They'd obviously been forewarned of my coming. People had seen me leave that morning, and while news travels fast on the coast, it obviously hadn't included my vices. So far on this trip, I'd been mistaken for a keep-fit maniac, a vegetarian, a social worker, a federal spy and an explorer with a death wish, but my vices have never been questioned. Cigarette lit, we then played out that ageless male tradition of marking one's territory.

For the uninitiated, there are three threads that bind together men who cross paths at sea. They are so thick and bright that even blind women can see them. They have no order, but are just like the secretive League of Masons', handshakes that carry messages and without which entry is forbidden. So it can be said, that similar rituals apply to men who meet at sea. They are......light up a cigarette, take a pee and talk sex.

I'd passed the first with flying colours, and no sooner had I inhaled my first drag, when I was holding onto my second. I felt edgy at first. There was little in the way of eye contact. They were checking out the newcomer, the upstart mainlander. Were they gleaning insights into my character, by the way I held myself? Maybe it was my fluid jet? the arc it made? its colour? or as I would like to believe, in my size? Whatever, they weren't disappointed and within minutes, we were talking sex.

It's strange how youth is wasted on the young; well, at least that day. We were three middle-aged men in boats, born into different cultures, and miles apart in lifestyles, talking of old conquests and ones just dreamed up in our heads. I had a great time, told my best lies, and left them thinking I'd impregnated every single woman on the coast. I was on a roll, and only one hour later, beached, adopted and sitting at a kitchen table in Tickle Cove, the stories only got better.

"There lad, it's a bit old, but it'll put hairs on your chest."

What's the chance of encountering three bears in one day? Sixty minutes before, I'd shared lies at sea with two huge grizzlies, and now I sat drinking fermented morning coffee from a chipped mug, in the presence of another called, Jim Kelly.

"It's a bit strong boy, but I'm sure it'll hit the spot."

Every nerve ending in my body was tingling with caffeine. I swore my toes curled and had I dropped my trousers, I'm sure my organ would have either burst into song, if not rose up and slapped me. To say that it was strong was putting it mildly. Beggars can't be choosers, but just as the first wave gripped my body, sending my senses into overdrive, he was topping it up again. I doubt if a line of cocaine could have had any more effect, and when he added a drop of rum, my body surrendered to the night.

I rose into the sun, paddled into the sun and for the first time since starting this trip, got well and truly fried by the sun. To say that the sea was hazy, was an understatement. The lighthouse at Little Denier hovered above the sea like a rocket on stilts; islands in front would sometimes float above water, connect themselves to the mainland, then spring back like rubber bands. Speedboats looked like longliners, and longliners' like colourful oil tankers, and thank God, the one and only iceberg I passed that morning, looked like one. I was beginning to think, I had eaten magic mushrooms for breakfast, and when a seal popped up and started talking in tongues, it was as if Christ himself had made an appearance. I never did catch up with my brain, and never made any sense out of the day. I was wasted, not from last night's drinks, but from the heat. It beat down like a red-hot hammer, reflected off the sea and wrapped around my body like a steaming towel. I was so tired, and dehydrated that I stopped at Puffin Island, and had it not been for the nauseating smell of bird chit, would have called it a day.

Newfoundland is an island of extremes, but I never expected in my wildest dreams, for it to be able to fry, me inside out. Now, to make matters worse, I was totally lost. The heat had played tricks with me while crossing Morris Channel. Its islands had united, only to break and shatter into points of land. It was getting increasingly difficult, not only to judge distances, but to focus on objects. The mid-day sun was wobbling and melting all before it, and it wasn't until my eyes latched onto a graveyard of crosses, and I turned down a channel into a blaze of colourful, albeit deserted, cabins, that I felt any sense of being grounded.

I couldn't buy a breeze for love nor money. It was so hot that even the mosquitoes were silent. I eventually put up my tent on a wooden slip, on Samson Flat Island, then climbed its shallow hill in search of a breeze.

Silence is a double-edged sword, but can be stunning if you embrace it. I rarely have problems with loneliness when surrounded by beauty, and the low-lying islands around Willis Reach in Bonavista Bay, under angled shadows of a setting sun, were spectacular. I love to rest my eyes on objects, caress them, stroke them, then fall back into my dreams, and the views that greeted me that evening, were more than enough to cuddle up to.

That night was one to savour. The sun set into a flaming red sky. The sea had stretched itself flat, and the chilled night air had taken away its halo of haze. That night drew me, like a curious child, into it. I stripped naked and walked on a deserted beach of powdered sand, with only the soft touch of a cool breeze for company; I was in heaven. The sea went from crimson to purple, then melted into liquid silver under a rising moon. Tomorrow would be a wonderful day. I just knew it.

That morning, the air and water were as one; crisp, still and opaque. My tent was dry as a bone. There was no morning dew, and already, I could feel the sun's heat. A lone speedboat chugged down the narrows, en route to Cottel Island, but no sooner had I popped my head out to greet it, when I was bushwhacked.

MOSQUITO ALERT........ small, pesky and as thirsty as hell. Needles on wings, as I like to call them, but as any hiker can testify, they are just smallfry compared to their big brothers, the BLACK FLIES. They came in waves. They got everywhere; in my ears, down my throat. I even felt them crawling down my neck and could almost imagine them abseiling down head hairs to eat my scalp. God, I hate them.

It is said that you can hit a black fly with a baseball bat and it will come back for more. They don't so much bite you, as mug you. When historians use the term, Canada's Untamed Wilderness, they aren't joking. Maybe the polar bear is king of the north, but even he wouldn't stand a chance against the relentless onslaught of the black fly. From July to September, there's only one creature that I'd bend my knee to, but sadly, on that day, even that didn't help. Black flies don't take prisoners. They eat until they drop, and until someone can provide evidence to the contrary, love the blood of Englishmen. They stuck to me like flies to chit, and it wasn't until a breeze picked up out to sea, that they finally left.

I can understand the nautical term, tickle and that arms and fingers of rock mean just what they say. A cape is a cape and a bay, a bay. Inlets, coves, narrows and sounds are words in common use, but what the hell is a Reach? In less than eighteen hours, I had traversed five of them, and now I was approaching yet another, called Lockers Reach. That morning was like a game of trivial pursuit and the term Reach, stuck to my head like crazyglue; that is, until my question was answered in the out-stretched arms of a mother, as she reaches for her child.... reach.... got it.

Anyone would be amazed at the unearthly cry of an humpback whale; that flute-like whine that she makes as if pulled through her soul, and it would be difficult to find anyone who doesn't love the haunting call of a loon, crying to her mate, but when you have heard and seen a dozen of both in an hour, it can wear a little thin. Sure, I'd crossed the paths of at least twenty pairs of loons and two humpbacks trying to mate, or were they kissing? I'd paddled past three icebergs, all big, all scarred in fissures of blue and green. One had even calved a chunk of ice the size of a pick-up truck, and I'd paddled through numerous tails of popping bergy bits. But that morning, it was the haze that catapulted my senses onto a different plane.

Have you ever seen Manhattan's skyline appear through a sea of haze? Well I have. The outport of Greenspond rose from the dead. I was still eight miles away from it, yet its houses looked like skyscrapers. A church, or was it a lighthouse, looked like the Empire State Building. A longliner floated by, as if on clouds, and a speedboat, like a silver streak. The heat was playing tricks with me. Colours overlapped, objects fell in and out of focus, and sounds stretched, then snapped like thunderclaps. Everything, except Greenspond ahead, was bleached in haze. The sea and sky were the colour of dull tin and the low-lying shore was lost to a wobbly curtain of heat. I am sure that if a three-headed Martian had materialized in front of me, I wouldn't have batted an eyelid. For two hours, I was in a world of my own, paddling, dreaming and soaking in the rays, and it wasn't until I entered Greenspond, that the spell was broken.

Chapter: 15
Family Tradition

"Fine craft me boy. Where you' longs to?"

Now this is a question with many answers. As a rolling stone, I had multiple choices; at Port-au-Port, I said Quebec, on the Southern Shore, Canada, and on a pub crawl in St. John's, when I told them Mud Lake, Labrador, it not only got me a drink, but the purchaser's sister. Today, I said England, the land of my birth, and immediately after the words popped out of my mouth, they were crossed by an invitation.

"Ya must come ta' lighthouse. Mind your mouth now. Wife's e'll be dere. She's making a jiggs dinner."

Jiggs dinner! It's one of my favourites. It was a family tradition. Sometimes, my mother made it with roast beef and sometimes, with the addition of salt pork. Just the thought of this meal made me drool. "Sure thing," I replied.

This is as good as it gets. I could hardly contain myself. Even though I'd sat down to eat with numerous families, and was certain I'd put on more weight than lost on this trip, I'd never been offered a jiggs dinner, or a bed in a light-house. That night, I didn't stray far from the kitchen table. I hovered around it like a hungry buzzard, looking for dessert, and was finally rewarded with cheesecake.

Jiggs Dinner
For the uninitiated, I downloaded this menu from the internet:

Preparation time: 30 minutes
Total time: 3 to 4 hours
Servings 6 to 8

Ingredients:
2 pounds of salt beef

1 cup of yellow peas
6 to 8 medium potatoes
6 carrots
1 medium turnip, peeled and cut in chunks
1 medium cabbage, cut in wedges
2 tablespoons of butter
Pepper to taste

Preparation:
1: Soak the meat (roast) in cold water overnight (6 - 8 hrs). Drain meat and place in a large pot.
2: Tie the peas in a cloth bag, leaving room for expansion, and put the bag in the pot with beef. Cover the peas and meat with water. Heat until boiled, cover and let it simmer for 2 hours.
3: Prepare the vegetables; small carrots and potatoes may be left whole, but cut the larger ones in half. Slice the turnip, and cut the cabbage into wedges.
4: After the meat and peas have cooked for 2 hrs, add the other vegetables and cook them, until they are tender, adding the cabbage last.
5: Remove the peas from the bag, place them in a bowl and mash them with butter and pepper to form what is called, peas pudding. Remove the meat and cut it into serving size slices.
6: Arrange the meat and vegetables on a platter. You serve the peas pudding in a separate bowl.
Newfoundlanders often pour the pot liquid (stock) over their dinner. The stock is also thickened for gravy to accompany the roast (moose, beef, chicken, caribou) that is also served at this meal.

Dawn couldn't come fast enough. The long-range weather forecast was calling for much of the same conditions for the next few days. I truly felt the worst was behind. I was ahead of schedule. My body was taught, belly stretched, and my head clear of all those worrisome thoughts of bay crossings. I could island-hop across Notre

Dame Bay, sprint if needed, across White Bay, and paddle around Hare Bay and St. John Bay if need be. While I'd given myself until the end of September to finish this trip, it was now looking like a mid-August finish.

They should rename Cape Freels to Cape Reef. To use the term, minefield of sunkers, for the seas in this area, was an understatement. One doesn't have too look to closely at a map to be able to read its shoreline. Lighthouses dotted this area, like bouncers at a policeman's ball, and we all know that reefs of rock attract beacons, like magnets attract metal filings. They were literally everywhere; Puffin Island, Partridge Island, Cabot Islands, Stevensons Islets, Bennets Island, Gull Island, plus numerous others on unnamed mastiffs of rock. At night, these waters must look like the Milky Way. In fact, the only point of land where there wasn't a lighthouse, was the low-lying cape itself.

Once past Greenspond, the mainland flattens like a pancake, but what a cake, and what a day to paddle in! A light wind wrinkled the sea. Cape Freels and her shoreline looked dusty and her nearby islands and exposed tidal rocks, dulled by the morning haze, looked like the freckled face of an Irishman. Only the lighthouses looked defined. They rose out of the sea like prairie grain elevators and dominated the horizon. Clouds smeared the sky like watercolours, and the sea looked barren. To break up my day and relieve boredom, I played games between rocks; a kind of childish touch-and-tell. I would try and get as close as possible to them, scooting between swells, and belting them with my paddle. The tide was falling, so I was forever watchful, but still, it was exhilarating. Waves were rolling and toppling all over the place. Occasionally, surf not strong enough to push me forward, rushed underneath and everywhere, sunkers were rising and falling with the ocean swells. Some waves would silently steepen, but wouldn't crest, while others curled unexpectedly from behind and required me to sprint out of their way. At one point, a mushroom of white exploded only yards away. A huge sunker rose into the sky, but luckily, the wave's suction prevented me from hitting it. My eyes were fixed in the direction that I was going and away from my boredom. On any other day, I would have given these rocks a wide birth, but in today's becalmed conditions, paddling in a lazy Atlantic swell was ideal for playing. For once, I could throw caution to the wind. I would paddle up to exposed sunkers, then wait, as if at a bus-stop, to be picked up. Some swells, forced up by submerged aprons of rock, were huge, and I glided effortlessly on them. It was exhilarating, and without this diversion, I would have been bored to death. I saw neither man nor beast that morning, and if not for the coastal road, would have spotted no one all day.

By late afternoon, I was ready to call it quits. I am not exactly superstitious, but who wants to make camp in a place called Dead Man's Bay, even if it is a provincial park with a reputedly glorious beach? Well, that should have been the least of my worries. I was tired, my forehead stung from sunburn, and I'd run out of water. I stubbornly ploughed on, even though my sea charts showed no signs of sheltered water for another five miles. Those squiggly, overlapping barbwire lines that denote shoal waters on sea charts, seemed to go on forever. I was almost at the limit of my endurance and at the point of turning back, when I saw a car parked at the top of a gut, with what looked like a small beach below.

When I am tired, I get careless. I had already allowed two large waves to carry me dangerously forward, towards some rocks. Straining and sitting bolt upright, I was trying to see a way through them, to the beach ahead. I edged forward, and with a crowd of onlookers to show off to, was getting downright dreamy. Why is it, that when I'm within spitting distance of shore, I feel like I can walk on water?

Suddenly, the bottom fell out of a wave. A rock appeared from nowhere and head-butted my kayak. The water kept falling and falling, until all I could see was rock. I had no idea that the water was so deep or the rock so big; then the inevitable happened. The sea roared back, raced up from below, and picked me up like a feather. One moment, I was breathing salt air and the next, salt water. It happened so quickly, I didn't even have chance to brace. My gelcoat was almost scraped clean. That beautiful repair job - well at least I though at the time - peeled off like dead skin. It is not speed that will wreck your kayak, but ego and complacency. Somehow, I managed to crawl back up the rock until I was level again, but no sooner was I upright, when another wave had me skidding towards the beach, like a toboggan at a fairground.

Too much alcohol, too warm a sleeping bag, and too many flies, combined to give me the worst night's sleep thus far on the trip. The friendly faces who witnessed me come ashore, insisted I share a drink, and once I'd checked my kayak and realized the sliver of fibreglass was not from the new repair job, but from an old patch-work of little consequence, I gave into celebration.

It's strange how the same rocks, viewed from the beach and paddled through at the beginning of the day, looked infinitely less intimidating than they did at yesterday's, day's end. It's so much easier to steer into waves and puncture them, than it is to be carried in their surf. Even though the sea was shrouded in early morning mist and under the influence of a moderate sea swell, I had no problem setting off that morning from the beach.

You may be starting to think that I was beginning to turn into an alcoholic and perhaps you're right. For sure, my earlier discipline was wavering. I wasn't exactly waking at dawn and kayaking until sunset. Just as marathon runners have pain barriers to pass through and second winds to be caught, the same can be said of long distance voyageurs. I was now well over halfway, if not physically, then mentally. I've made enough of these trips to know when the writing is on the wall, and know enough about myself not to worry about it too much. Sometimes it's good to abuse your body and let off steam. I was ripe for a little foolishness, so when I encountered two fishermen in the waters around Ladle Cove, I easily gave in to their invitation. "You must drop-in and see Erick West. He's built his own kayak."

Erick is what I would call a weekend paddler, with a difference; he loves it. If I could be classed as the wild man of paddling, then Erick would be my intellectual twin. Quiet to the point of submissiveness, willowy, and wearing horn-rimmed glasses, he wouldn't have looked out of place on a university campus, and like so many educated people of his generation who didn't give into the seduction of mainland culture, was a traditionalist.

What is a traditionalist? Someone rooted; someone with a sense of place. To sustain traditions, you must have a strong attachment to both land and family, and Erick had both in spades. Born into a tradition of Newfoundland politics before Confederation, he was drenched in it. I have traveled from coast to coast, so I cannot honestly say that Newfoundland had cornered the market on these values. Afterall, Quebec's traditions are guarded by language, and other places in Canada like Labrador and the Yukon, by their remoteness, but nowhere else, have I found this sense of attachment to a place and family, with such gale force intensity as on the Rock.

And so it was that Bernie - the lover of tradition, with all its warts and pimples - would spend the next few days bouncing from one engagement to the next, drinking and eating and generally making a complete ass of himself.

My diary of events during those days is a little sketchy. I know I ate crab, moose and barbeque ribs, and drank at least two bottles of wine, helped drain a twelve ouncer of rum and a six-pack of beer. In between, I hitchhiked to Caramanville to pick up some mail, and ended up spending the night with Marilyn and John Tulk. I remember meeting a dear friend of mine, David Zelser, the only C.B.C. television interviewer that I would give the time of day to, let alone be recorded to be gawked at on the evening news. I remember meeting Judy, and her fork feeding me scallops, as if I was a nesting bird. Those days were needed to unwind, and when I finally turned the page on wine, women and song, I left in overdrive.

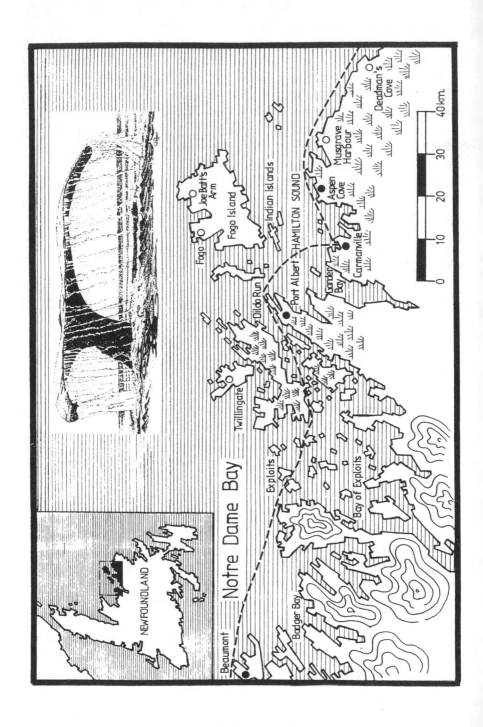

Chapter: 16
Notre Dame Bay

I have this unwritten rule that I rarely break while traveling. It reads, "Once you've turned the page, there's no turning back." That's why I never did set foot on Fogo Island, but it's also the reason, I found another, called Exploits, in Notre Dame Bay.

When I think of Newfoundland's fisheries, boat building heritage and resettlement, the first name that pops into my head, is Fogo Island. From school, I knew its topography, rugged coastline, and the stories behind the names of Fogo and Joe Batt's Arm, almost as well as those of my own birthplace. So you can imagine my disappointment when plans to see the source of all this rich history flew out of the window with the wind, but a rule is a rule.

The day had started off well enough. A light tailbreeze pushed me across Gander Bay, en route towards Hamilton Sound. My planned route that morning, was to island-hop; Gander Island to Dog Bay Island, to Western Indian Island, then to Stag Harbour on Fogo Island. But as soon as Stag Tickle came into view, a strong northeasterly set in. I just couldn't buy any progress for love nor money. It went from light to gale force within minutes. It was as if the gods were stripping Fogo from my hands, as though they were asking for a sacrifice. For thirty minutes, I paddled like a madman, but I just couldn't gain a toehold down the tickle. It was blowing so hard, that surf was atomizing in the wind and being carried like white-hot pellets. My eyes were red and raw in no time, and my wrists didn't bear thinking about. I was never in any physical danger, as the conditions were only localised, but definitely, my stubborn streak was flirting with insanity.

The moment I turned with the wind, is the moment I knew I'd never set foot on Fogo; that she'd been my sacrifice, and true to my nature, once my back was turned, she was lost to me.

Ironically, that night I found myself camped at the foot of Farewell Harbour, watching the Fogo Island passenger ferry steam to and fro. The gods, having accepted my decision to by-pass Fogo and take Dildo Run, now smiled on me. The wind died that night, the seas stretched taut and the waters around my camp turned into a colourful nesting ground for sea ducks.

That morning, I woke into an enormous appetite. Normally, my breakfast consists of the two ines, caffeine and nicotine, but having accepted my fate to miss out on Fogo, I decided to visit the ferry terminal for a bite to eat.

When I was a kid, there was a radio program called, Talking Heads. It was based on regional dialects. Street corner conversations were taped and then played back in front of a studio panel of educated people. They were all asked to guess what the conversations were about. Invariably, they all guessed wrong, but the program was hilarious. That morning, sitting down and eating a morning breakfast of spam and eggs, I became the unwitting listener to a similar, albeit live, Talking Heads, program. The invited guests were two American tourists, discussing communication skills.

Some people find the Newfie accent as foreign to them as French. Some use it as a reason for never stepping out of St. John's. I say, poppycock. For me, that's the glory of foreign travel. I don't want to know what people are talking about all of the time. I can't think of anything that excites a greater sense of childlike wonder, than to be in a country where you're ignorant of almost everything. Suddenly, you're five years old again. You can't read anything. You only have the most rudimentary sense of how things work, and can't even reliably cross a street without endangering your life. Your whole experience becomes a series of interesting guesses, and at that very moment, I wished that I was in the Americans' shoes, as they were having the time of their lives.

The men were from Maine; Boston, actually. To them, the printed ferry schedule was as it is; not printed on stone, but with room for change. Since arriving, they'd been rained on, fogged in, and blown flat on their faces, yet everyday had been a "Fine Day", as they're called in Newfoundland. If they had wanted sun, they would have gone to Florida. I loved eavesdropping on their conversation and reveled in the attempted pronunciation of such everyday sayings, as........

Dn't da fulish bye - isn't that foolish, boy.
Give us a bitta dat luv - give us a bit of that, love.
Garnteed, b'y - I agree.
Shut up your prat - be quiet.

.........from their Newfie Dictionary. I would have loved to join in, but sometimes it's better to leave things alone.

I was now used to psychoanalyzing myself by using a forecaster's weather report; rained in = depression; strong northeasterlies = grounded; sunny and clear = life couldn't be better. Today, it was a touch of sunny with cloudy periods = no problemo, but then I didn't take Dildo Run into consideration.

The moment I turned down Dildo Run and saw its maze of islands, was the moment I knew I'd made a mistake. It was like looking down the throat of a lush green ice-jam. Newfoundland may be on your left, to an anti-clockwise paddler, but down Dildo Run, it comes at you from all directions. To say its navigation was a challenge, was putting it mildly. I got totally confused. It was hard to judge where one island ended and another began. In places, it was so shallow, so full of seaweed, that it was like poling across a bowl of porridge. Sometimes a current would pick up. I'd squeeze between some rocky outcrop, then float over green ribbons of seagrass as if flying through clouds, but there was a silver lining. I saw numerous crabs, shoals of small fish and more than half a dozen families of playful sea otters.

The day's paddle would have been easy, had I not lost sight of a marker buoy. I'd been leap-frogging from one to the other, but the sight of a speedboat had sucker-punched me into taking another route; now I was paying the penalty. In the end, I ran out of water, down a deadend channel, and had I not seen a car whiz by above its banks, I might still have been there.

Thank God, Newfoundlanders plan for the worst and hope for the best, because from a distance, I'm sure that in my skin tight wet suit, I must have looked like a distraught transvestite. I hadn't even stuck my thumb out, but was standing in the middle of the road, trying to work out what the body of water was, on the other side. I knew that a bridge spanned Dildo Run somewhere, but where, was anyone's guess.

"Are ya lost me b'ye?"

I'd not even noticed that a car had stopped, but when its driver stepped out, I was gob-smacked.

Wow!!! Just my type; rough and ready with an Eskimo's full-face smile and eyes to die for. It helped that she had a shock of red hair that curled to her shoulders and a workman's kneecap sweater. At that moment, I would have sold my mother as a galley slave and plunged a dagger into my thigh for her, then I saw her wedding band.

"You must be Bernie. I saw ya yesterday on the C.B.C. Where's ya kayak?"

What are the odds of meeting not one, but three beautiful women in one day? To hell with kayaking! I was beginning to take to this roadside cruising, for within minutes of our introduction, she'd not only helped me portage my kayak across the road, but introduced me to Dirk Muir, a come-from-away Springbok, and two more girls.

Later, having beached my kayak adjacent to the road in someone's back garden, Dirk and the girls gave me a lift into Twillingate, where we all spent a pleasant evening eating and drinking together. It was great for once, to relax in the company of females, to be able to flirt and dance the dance, but that night belong to Dirk.

In Dirk, I found a fellow immigrant, a transplanted South African who had fallen, like myself, under the Rock's spell.

What is it I wonder, that makes immigrants either love or hate the Rock? There seems to be no inbetween. I used to call it the born again syndrome. Dirk, like myself, had embraced Canada and especially the Rock, faults and all, but unlike myself, he'd taken it one step further. He owned a piece of it, and before paddling away the next morning, I promised to meet up with him and the girls at his renovated cottage on Exploits Island.

As bays go, Notre Dame Bay, and the seas around Exploits in particular, were the most kayaking friendly waters I'd paddled to date. In Exploits Island, with its dominating Man-of-War Hill, narrow tickle and iggily-piggily, ramshackled terraces of picturesque summer cottages, I found a settlement that could pluck the strings of any heart. That night, on Exploits, I sat down, eating supper with Dirk and the girls, under a setting sun. I felt totally relaxed. The girls were animated, friendly and funny. Dirk provided the wine and it flowed freely. I was mellow, without a care in the world. Not for the first time, I felt like jumping ship and making the harbour where I now stood, my home. Exploits Island has everything that a writer like myself requires; a room with a view, weekend visitors and volumes of silence. That night, I gave into my dreams of the future, putting down roots, buying a speedboat and making the Rock my home.

I enjoyed the traverse of Notre Dame Bay more than all the other bays put together. It was intimate, full of incident and for once, the weather was accommodating throughout. West of Exploits, islands rose out of the sea in gigantic mushrooms of rock. Distant icebergs hovered over the horizon, and as I approached one close to home, it split into two columns like the Parthenon in Athens. The whole bay reminded me of the coastline of Labrador, of its silver seas and blue rocks. At Fortune Hill, I beached and climbed into a spectacular view. Longliners, fishing in clusters, looked like armadas of colour; eagles spiraled, and puffins and gannets burst into view, in clouded wheels of motion. The morning drifted. I hit a rhythm early, relaxed in the heat and glided more than paddled, then.....

I got the shock of my life near Woody Island. I saw five plumes of vapour, five black-bladed dorsal fins. They were killer whales, traveling fast and coming in my direction. Some people say these whales can swim over twenty knots. I could only guess at their speed, but I swore they were hydroplaning.

Where the hell did the pod of Orcas come from? I thought that they were Pacific mammals, not Atlantic. Maybe they were lost, got their antennas crossed. Maybe global warming was the reason, but whatever the reason, at that moment, I thought myself the bait, and began paddling as if my life depended on it.

Within seconds, my arms took on a life of their own. They started rotating like supercharged windmills and didn't stop until I'd attached myself to a marker buoy. I swear I was in tears. I hovered around the buoy, as if my life depended on it. I'd not been so frightened in ages. Although they are the darlings of Greenpeace, ECO Tourism, and have their images printed on everything from chocolate bar wrappers to beer labels, they are not my kettle of fish.

I have never read or heard reports of incidents involving Orcas and kayakers, but I certainly didn't want to be the first, and when one popped up only yards from the buoy, I nearly freaked out. I swear that at that instant, I would have blown it to smithereens if I'd had a cannon. Some people think they are beautiful, the lions of the seas, but I hate those dorsal fins. They cut through the water like a knife through butter, and I hear that their razor-sharp teeth could do the same with flesh. Perhaps I'd seen too many re-runs of Jaws. Once in Vancouver, I'd been told that in the mammal world, their intelligence and agility was unrivaled, that they had a cat's cunning, the patience of Jobe, and a sadistic streak, bar none. Even from the safety of the Vancouver Island Ferry, they'd looked creepy. Today, exposed at sea, they looked downright terrifying.

I was about one mile out from the nearest point of land, and felt about as buck-naked and defenseless against these whales, as a nudist facing a gang of armed terrorists. A video image of a two thousand pound sea lion, knocked senseless, passed around like a basketball amongst the pod, then being devoured, had burned into my brain. It was stuck on rewind. The sea was blood red. The Indians are coming!...the Indians are coming!....Where's John Wayne when you want him?......then the cavalry arrived

"Have you seen the Orcas?"

Have I seen Orcas! I wanted to jump up and kiss him full on the mouth. I've never been so glad to see a speedboat full of tourists in all my life. My jaw flapped open, but words failed to fall out. I could only point, stare and hope for the best. "Cheers......see ya," and they were gone.

I stayed, glued to the buoy for another ten minutes. I was still in shock. Seeing the pod up close, had made me feel small, very small, and this feeling stayed with me for the rest of the day.

It was early evening before I turned my thoughts to a campsite. I chose, a small sheltered bay within earshot of Beaumont, Long Island, on the western reaches of Notre Dame Bay. It was a gentle beach, hemmed in by a rocky scree at the bottom of a grassy slope; flowers were in full bloom, yellow-button holed white daisies carpeted all rises, and iris and bluebells stuck between its rocks. The small hill behind, opened onto another bay. This was the camp I was hoping to find; sufficiently exposed to avoid the flies, a nice view of the sea, and adequately sheltered by surrounding hills, in case of a storm. I beached in a shower, put up my tent under a rainbow and ate under the sun. Later that evening, the soundness of my choice was confirmed by a beautiful multi-coloured sunset, and when the pod of Orcas appeared again, viewed from solid ground it was a perfect ending to the day..... and what a day!

I woke into an early morning heat haze. The sea was again glass calm and the rugged coastline up to Cape St. John was just amazing. There was no rush. I'd heard of a small, resettled fishing community called Round Harbour, on the Baie Vert Peninsula, and wanted to explore it. I could have followed the bay's perimeter, kept close to land and explored its outer reaches, but the open sea was just too inviting. At 10:00 am, I broke camp, was approaching Snooks Head by 1:00 pm, and found myself paddling through a crack in rock by 2:00 pm.

Can things get any better? It had been a question that was uppermost in my thoughts all morning. Notre Dame Bay, with its cliffs of bald rock, islands skirted in scree, and heads of lush green forest, was worth the price of admission. Most of all, these vistas as seen through the window of cloudless skies had been awesome. All of these views had been natural wonders, but even Exploits, as pretty as it was, lacked that all inspiring wild and worn-in look I had expected to find in an old fishing community. What Exploits lacked however, Round Harbour, viewed through its splintered opening in rock, had in spades.

Round Harbour, until recent times, could only be accessed by the sea. Built around a steep and naturally horseshoe shaped inlet, on a narrow-fingered peninsula just north of Snooks Arm, it could easily be missed. The community, stuck as if by crazyglue to steep rock, and tiered down to stilted fishing stages, looked every bit like the communities of old. I'd even researched it on the internet before leaving Sept-Isle. It had been settled, like many on the coast, by only a few families in the mid 1800's. In those days, the fishing grounds off Cape St. John had been excellent. Like so many deserted outports, its original homes had been built for single fishermen, then extended to house their families. It had evolved over time and population, into a year-round community, with church, school and store. In its heyday in the early 1900's, it was home to two hundred people, then declined with the fisheries.

I counted maybe thirty livable homes clinging to its rocky shores. Some of these houses were the old style, with narrow clap-board, small windows and narrow, pitched roofs, but most it seems to be the norm in these old communities, have been renovated, or in some cases, completely built from scratch. The earliest families to arrive in the harbour, clearly got the best sites, whilst late arrivals were forced to homestead around the sides, closer to its narrow entrance. I was told that the young family's house that guards the harbour's entrance, had been washed away at least once, and twice during winter storms had been evacuated. Only recently, had a road reached through to the harbour. The gravel road had given it a new lease on life, a blood transfusion, and you didn't have to be a rocket scientist to see from the steep inclines that it could only be used in summer and without it, this community of less than fifty souls would surely die.

That night, I chose a fishing stage to camp on and had a beautiful night. For once, I kept to myself. I did get an invite, but declined. It's strange, going in and out of civilization; one night camped under the stars, the next, under roof, one night eating freeze-dried food balanced on your knees and the next, a home-cooked meal from a kitchen table. Some days, I crave the sounds of lapping water and the open-air call of sea gulls, and on others, the T.V. remote. It's both seductive and repellent, to sink into the comfortable ambiance of family life, to have the sun set at the flick of a switch, set your own comfort level by thermostat and enjoy the feel of clean linen on a showered body. It makes me lazy. In Exploits, I chose my tent over Dirk's guest room, and yesterday, a secluded beach over a home invitation in Beaumont. It's difficult to change clothes on the fly, adjust table manners, and always be up for your audience. My public persona was wearing a little thin, my politician's smile, a little jaded. I made a promise to myself that night, to camp more and accept fewer night's between clean sheets.

Cape St. John.....now that's a man's cape; great slabs of vertical rock. One gets dizzy just looking up, and God help a hatching sea gull that suffered vertigo. What a rock face; what a sky and what a day!

In Manful Bight, my path crossed that of the caplin fishery; two boats anchored in a lazy swell, a handwave followed by, "Fine day for paddling, boy," and within minutes, I was feasting in their presence.

Most land lovers are amazed that I've paddled so far, and only a few have viewed my trip as a recreation or an escape, but fishermen are a breed unto themselves, and they are no respecters of bullshit. On shore, I've heard comments as diverse as, "ya crazy" to "good on ya boy". Some have been vaguely displeased, jealous even, but most have made me feel proud of my achievement. But without exception, the only viewpoint that interests me, is the one offered out at sea.

Fishermen are fishermen wherever they work, whether it be on a factory boat, the family longliner, or hauling lobster traps from a speedboat. They all stand on water, and I think it's this common bond that gives me and my trip, instant credibility. Maybe it's this, or as I would like to think, that storms are great levelers - waves do not discriminate - they can just as easily snap an oil tanker in two, as capsize a kayak. It's just as easy to drown within hailing distance of land, as it is over the horizon. I really have no idea why the Newfoundland fishermen took to both me and my trip, but one thing is for certain, memories of these coastal encounters, of our shared experiences on her waters, will stay with me long after this book has been published.

I stayed, shooting the breeze for as long as I dared. The

sun's glare had softened, a dampness had fallen, and as I paddled away from the boat, thick clouds of fog began blotting out the cape's point.

I made La Scie in a drizzle, erected my tent in a shower and ate in a downpour. That night, the rain whipped my tent, but I didn't care. Cocooned in a warm sleeping bag and reading under candlelight, Bernie was a happy camper. Even when the skies lit up and crackled with thunder, I couldn't care less. My tent was brilliant. It was into its third long trip in eight years, (Moss Inc., Stardomed 11, all season tent) and except for two patches, was almost as good as new. It had been a sponsorship freebie, and together with my six year old kayak, (Current Designs, Solstice GT) the only other freebie to stand the test of time. I am not a believer in sponsorship. We had a saying when I was a lad, "You don't get 'owt for n'owt," which roughly translated, means, "You don't get anything for nothing in this life." I have always treated sponsorship as a bonus, but have never been a slave to it.

I have these golden rules, I never break and use them as guidelines when planning a trip. They are:
1: If you cannot afford to take a trip without sponsorship, you shouldn't take it.
2: Allow yourself an open-ended return ticket. If a trip looks like it will take three months, then plan on four. Haste, not weather, is the major killer. If your hands are tied because of time constraints, make sure your life insurance policy is paid up-to-date before leaving.
3: I have always planned for the worst and hoped for the best, and I never cut corners when it comes to money. Details have never interested me; my clothes are nearly all second-hand and a paddle is a paddle. The only things I spare no expense on, are kayak, tent and sleeping bag.
4: Last, but not least, I always try to eat the best freeze-dried food on the market. Weight, for a lean person like myself, is a problem. I start to eat and drink like a pig, for at least six weeks before a trip. I try to put on an extra layer of fat, ten

pounds if possible.

It was your typical,"fog some tick me boy," kind of morning. It was that thick, I could hardly see my hand in front of
my face. Leaving wasn't an option, but staying in my tent
seemed no better either. Then a fishplant worker dropped
by, and I was adopted. One thing led to another, first a sit-
down breakfast, then a guided tour of his fishplant.

The fishplant, like so many others, had been converted
from fish to shrimp. By-products are now the name of the
game, and the Japanese yen is quickly becoming the currency of choice. That afternoon, on my guided tour, I reveled in being centre stage, playing up to the cat-calls about
my hair net and flirting with the female plant workers. Later,
I was given the keys to the town's library, spent hours
answering emails, and in the evening, helped my newfound
friend empty a bottle of wine.....how sweet life is.

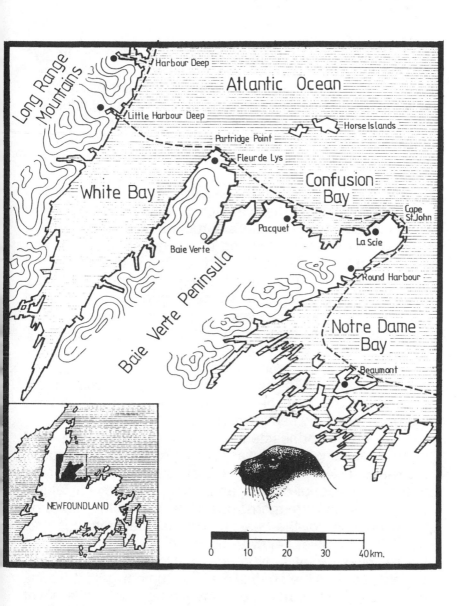

Long Range Mountains

Harbour Deep

Atlantic Ocean

Little Harbour Deep

Horse Islands

Partridge Point

Fleur de Lys

Confusion Bay

White Bay

Cape St. John

Pacquet

La Scie

Baie Verte

Round Harbour

Baie Verte Peninsula

Notre Dame Bay

Beaumont

NEWFOUNDLAND

0   10   20   30   40 km.

Chapter: 17
Fog - Fog - Fog

Not again........When you least expect, it the sea throws you a curve ball.

There's a good reason why the bay I was paddling, is called Confusion Bay. It is a veritable dictionary of tidal rips, cross-currents and reflective waves. Then throw into that mix, its underwater mountain ranges and a strong, early evening northeasterly, and you have a recipe called confused seas.

By late afternoon, the fog had lifted from La Scie, and by early evening, I was halfway across Confusion Bay. I had what I thought was Pacquet's harbour beacon in my sights, but I wasn't too sure. My sea chart was soaking wet and impossible to pry open without shredding in the wind. I had been forced into using my 1:250,000 topographical map and was trying to make an educated guess, never a good thing to do in clapping waves. In short, I was paddling blind. I was angling over slowly, to a knuckle of rock, topped by a beacon. The rock was split from the land, but its narrow channel looked far from being sheltered. Howling winds carried airborne surf, as if dust from a gravel road. I just couldn't believe that the channel ahead was the harbour entrance, but if it wasn't, where was it?

The strong northeasterly was pushing me towards land at an astounding pace. I was running out of options, but as the island rock slipped away, the exposed channel seemed to widen. It was, of course, an illusion, a bloody, awful illusion. The seas were monstrous. Now, I knew that I was on the wrong side of the beacon. The harbour entrance was now clearly visible, below Cape Brule, on the other side of the half hidden inlet. Maybe I was just to lazy to turn around, paddle back into the open sea and circumnavigate the rock, but turning back is not one of my strong points. I've never liked facing rough seas in strong winds. It's not that I am a risk-taker, but if I am going to paddle through dangerous waters, I'd rather do it behind a rock with land in sight, than in front of one in open sea.

I must have burned a thousand calories of nervous energy, watching surf bubble and boil in the turbulent waters of the channel, but no sooner had I made up my mind to take it on, when my brain switched to my reserve tank.

Wow! Once I'd made that decision, my body slipped a few gears into overdrive. What an adrenalin rush! What a ride, and what an end to the day.

I rose into fog the next morning, broke camp in the fog and left in the fog. My tent was saturated. I debated whether to stay in Pacquet, wait until the sun burned its way through and dried my tent, but I only planned to paddle fifteen miles that day. Before attempting to cross White Bay the next day, I wanted to spend the night at Fleur-de-Lys, at the tip of the Baie Verte Peninsula.

This bay wouldn't be my last crossing, but the last of any consequence. I wanted to cross it in the early hours of the morning. White Bay is known for its funneling winds, and its mountainous Northern Peninsula for generating strong, late afternoon downdrafts. Both Little and Greater Harbour Deep, at the other side of the bay, were known for these winds. I had already battled against these downdrafts before. They could appear suddenly, last minutes or hours, and I knew, I didn't posses the upper body strength to fight a prolonged battle against them. Dantzic Point's cornering winds had tested my physical endurance to its limits. Fighting a battle against 50 knot winds, within a stone's throw from land is one thing, to endure them face-on in open sea, maybe three miles from shore, is as different as chalk and cheese. It was Newfoundland's coastal winds, not its rocks, that I'd been warned about, especially by a lobster fisherman that I met at Port-au-Port.

"Rocks me boy. We got lots of those." I'd asked him about some rocks ahead." In fact, we've got thousands of 'em... washbowls, sunkers. We got one called Needles, further down the coast, then there's Long Harry, Table Top. I could go on all day if tha wants." Then, he turned his attention to my kayak. "Eh lad, in that thing ya don't need to know." He wasn't the first fisherman to roll his eyes at the sight of my boat. "I think what ya wonna know is if ya sane. On a day like today, you've no problem, even if ya bottom out, but if the wind blows, I wouldn't want to be in that thing, even if tha pays me. It's not the rocks you have to worry about, me boy, it's the wind, and I don't mean that stuff ya hears about on the radio. It's those shifty ones; the ones that prowl around, then vanish, the ones that hide behind clouds, lay in wait, down coves. It's those buggers that drop down cliffs and crush ya.....Take for instance, Blow-me-Down..... He really didn't have to go any further. He was talking to the converted. That's why today, I was taking every precaution possible, by going only as far as Fleur-de-Lys, before crossing White Bay tomorrow.

I guess I was paying the price for the last five days of calm weather. The inland skies were oppressive; mottled grey clouds were hanging low and the shoreline ahead was obscured by fog. That morning, everything looked dark and uninviting. I started hugging the shoreline from the word go, but still, it was hit and miss. At Point Rousse, the land slipped away into infinity and the fog rolled in. For the next sixty minutes, I paddled blind, with only the noise of my own thoughts for company, then..... woosh!

Thank God for the cluster of rocks, called, The Sisters. I heard them, long before I saw them. How many gulls were grounded on their rocks, I have no idea, but the sound that they made as I approached, was deafening. I was on top of them before they sensed my presence, but when they did, they appeared out of the gloom, as if shot from a gattling gun. They were a welcome sight; in fact, anything that morning would have been welcome.

I reached Fleur-de-Lys as the fog lifted, ate and drank sundowners with the family whose land my tent was pitched on, then rolled over into a dreamless sleep.

Give me a break! It wasn't the fog this time, but the wind. Take away the bay's turbulent sea, and the view across White Bay - with its razor edged mountains and its awesome, unbroken line of 1000 foot cliffs - was magnificent, but that morning, I wasn't into mountain climbing. The funnelling winds were rafting the bay's tidal currents and surf streaked its water, like a snakepit of angry serpents.

I had woken to a cloudless sky, but the morning rays were deceptive. The hills surrounding Fleur-de-Lys, had baffled the wind to such a degree, it felt breathless. The view east was becalmed, but once I'd rounded Partridge Point and been slapped by its cornering winds, I knew better. Once again, I had to play the game of patience and wait out the wind. I beached, pulled up my kayak above the tide, erected my tent and fell asleep.

When will I ever learn? Obviously, not that day. The crossing had started with a tailwind. I'd just been passed by a longliner and had stopped. I was taking in the scene ahead, enjoying a coffee and relaxing into a smoke, when the wind picked up. It was 6:00 pm.

To underline the day's conditions, I have inserted my website's entry, dated;

July 28th:
Give me a break -White Bay

Today, I paid the penalty for five unbroken days of ideal paddling conditions. Notre Dame Bay had both smiled and toasted me, with hardly a hint of ripple. Even the intimidating miles of rock that make up Cape St. John and its reputedly turbulent waters, were sleeping when I rounded them. In fact, I was getting complacent. I was starting to wake later and finish earlier, but all went terribly wrong, the day I crossed the 16 miles of open water across White Bay.

I had done all the right things leading up to the crossing. I had camped the night before at the bay's closest settlement at Fleur-de-Lys. I woke at the crack of dawn, went down to the wharf to get the marine weather forecast, which not for the first time on this trip, turned out to be incorrect - then set-off.

I was at Partridge Point by 9:00 am, but the sight that greeted me across the bay to Great Harbour Deep - my planned destination on the Northern Peninsula - wasn't a pretty one. The forecasted light winds were funnelling down the bay at gale force and the sea was boiling. I beached in a small cove, put up my tent, set my alarm clock for 2:00 pm and catnapped. Sure enough, the winds died.

By 3:00 pm, I was in the water and by 6:00 pm, within two miles of the far shoreline. I had actually sprinted across. Taking a break, I was having a cup of coffee from my flask and had just lit up a cigarette, when the wind picked up again, flipped ninety degrees, and started to funnel down the fjord-like inlet that I was facing. Out here, they call them downdrafts. It's when hot air starts to cool in the mountains, falls, picks up speed in the inlets, and heads back out to sea at gale force. It's not that I thought I was going to capsize; it wasn't that type of wind. It came at you head on, forty to fifty knots. It just wore you down. It took me over two and a half hours to paddle the two miles to the shoreline, then the extra three miles down the inlet to the only life I could see at Little Harbour Deep.

Thank God, the morning's heavy winds had grounded two crab fishermen, Little Harbour Deep's only summer residents from going out to their pots, because I don't know what I would have done without them. I arrived on the beach in front of their camp, spent, cold and wet. My eyes were stinging from the salt water spray; the palms of my hands were raw from gripping my paddle, and my wrists felt like fused joints. The light was fading fast behind the mountains, and I must have looked a rare sight to them as I came ashore. I was not really in a fit state to put up my tent, let alone cook an evening meal and when I fell out of my kayak on the beach, it must have told them something because that night, Tom and Lee came to my rescue. They gave me freshly smoked sea trout and then some home-brew to wash it all down.

I am now at the foot of the Northern Peninsula, three quarters of the way around Newfoundland. Tomorrow, I start the long haul up to St. Anthony. Just three more weeks.........

I left Little Harbour Deep in a sorry state. First, two fingers on each hand were bent closed and needed popping out, but they weren't the only things not answering the morning bell. My knees were shot and my legs had short-circuited and took on lives of their own. My face, reflected in the washroom mirror, half hidden behind three days of stubble, looked sickening, and with my bent over gate, I looked like the hunchback of Notre Dame with an attitude. Everything, if not looking crooked, felt like it, but thank God, my plumbing was in working order, if not its sense of direction.

That morning, I didn't so much jump-start my body into action, as coax it. To say I felt fragile and delicate, was putting it mildly. When you're over 50, you don't bounce back like a yoyo, as you did in your teenage years. I felt every day of my age and then some. Even my time-tested morning medication of coffee and cigarettes didn't work, and I'd almost paddled the fifteen miles to Great Harbour Deep, before feeling human.

I didn't really want to visit Great Harbour Deep, and had I not needed to pick up my mail, certainly wouldn't have. Great Harbour Deep is situated over five miles down an inlet. It seemed to go on forever, and even when its harbour came into view, its wharf just kept falling away from me. I was kicking myself for not looking at my map before choosing its post office as my general delivery address. Entering the harbour, I was so tired, so spent, that even if a naked mermaid had surfaced, I couldn't have saluted her, and God help me if a boatload of Playgirl Bunnies invited me for supper. I was empty, gone, finished. I was in the land of goblins, an Alice in Wonderland of hallucinations fed by fatigue, and no sooner had I tied up to someone's stage, when I was sleeping under canvas, dead to the world.

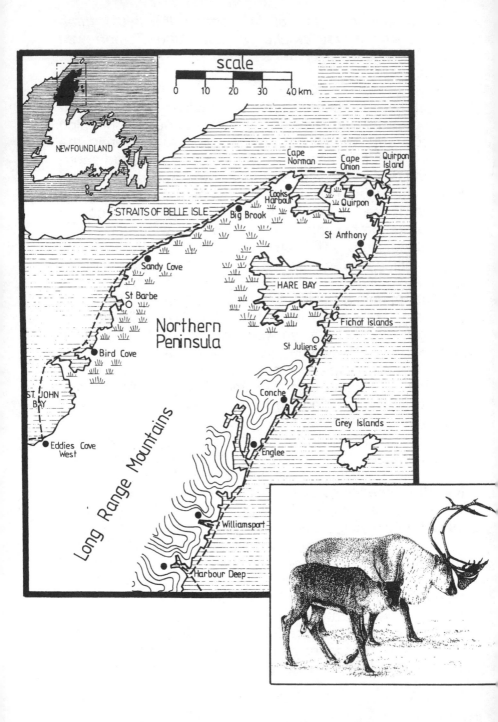

scale

0 10 20 30 40 km.

NEWFOUNDLAND

STRAITS OF BELLE ISLE

Cape Norman

Cape Onion

Quirpon Island

Cooks Harbour

Big Brook

Quirpon

St Anthony

Sandy Cove

St Barbe

HARE BAY

Northern Peninsula

Fichot Islands

St Juliens

Bird Cove

ST. JOHN BAY

Conche

Grey Islands

Eddies Cove West

Englee

Long Range Mountains

Williamsport

Harbour Deep

Holy Smoke! Nothing like being woken by the devil on Sunday. There are only two places on this planet, with the savvy to play piped gospel music as a call to Sunday morning prayer; Newfoundland and Nashville. I've traveled the world and heard wailing mullahs with vocal chords the equal of any top class baritone, belting out the Qur'an from mosques as far afield as Pakistan and Indonesia. I've heard church bells playing playful tunes all over Europe, and I've listened to the himalayas come to life in the echoed tones of Buddhist trumpets from mountaintop monasteries, but you haven't lived, until you have heard Johnny Cash wailing through fog.

Since rigormortis had set in, I never did get to church. If I'd knelt, I'd never stand again. For once, I was glad to be fogbound. I stayed curled up in my sleeping bag and played catch-up. I slept most of the morning glued to my tent, and blissfully ignorant of my trip. I dreamed in technicolour and the only movements I made, were from hand to mouth, and it was only when I ran out of chocolate bars, that I ventured out.

In for a penny, in for a pound. When you're up, you're up, and when you're out, you're out. Maybe I'd been paddling for too long, for no sooner had my blood started to circulate, when I was packed and paddling away...in afternoon fog.

Yoooooooooh............Yoooooooooh

Oooops....A humpback was in the vicinity, and looking for trouble.

My imagination was playing tricks with me. I had this vision of seeing an oversexed male appearing out of the fog, rearing out of the water, seeing a penis the size of a city block heading in my direction, and feeling ten tons of blubber crashing down on my head. This was not going to be a pretty sight. What would they write on my tombstone? Lost at sea or raped? I picked up my rhythm, paddled out of earshot, then made a mental note to paint tiger stripes on my kayak's belly..... a bizaare idea, but then I have a bizaare imagination.

The fog has mixed blessings. The obvious disadvantage is that it shuts down one's vision, but the advantage is that it baffles the wind. Another day, paddling in another place, I would never have ventured out in my kayak, but today's coastline rose straight out of the sea. I didn't have shoal waters to worry about, nor sunkers and there wasn't a hope in hell of encountering a longliner. There's a saying in Newfoundland, "the thicker the fog, the lighter the wind," and I can testify to its validity. There was a sea swell, but no wind found its way through the fog. I generally kept to a north by northeast setting and only got lost once, at Pigeon Cove, where I mistook it for another cove. I never did get to see the Northern Peninsula's mountains, and only glimpsed its vertical wall of cliffs below their ankles.

I made the old whaling station of Williamsport, a few hours before sunset. The fog had lifted its hemline slightly, but still, visibility was at a premium, and when I spotted two yachts, anchored close to shore, I hooked my eyes to their portholes and reeled myself up to them.

To say I was apprehensive at meeting their occupants, was putting it mildly. I still find it hard to shake my English 'working class' roots. I am Canadian by choice, but still English by birth, and old prejudices are hard to let go. There's a fine line between snobbery and its reverse cousin, when viewed from the bottom of the totem pole. The yachts looked magnificent, tall and imposing from a kayaker's point of view. I only had one thing on my mind that evening, and that was to find out tomorrow's weather, then get the hell out of their faces, but sometimes, first impressions can be lightyears away from the truth.

At first glance, the yacht's tinted windows carried an attitude of celebrity, isolation and aloofness. It's easy for a kayaker to forget that the elements spray us all equally; the weather can crack and leather the skin of both rich and poor alike, storms can humiliate both strong and weak, and regardless of the bulk of the craft, it's the person who stands on it, that counts. It's easy to forget that when you are at the bottom of the ladder, not everything is hunky-dory at the top.

They adopted me almost immediately, and within minutes of my stepping aboard, were sharing both their evening meal and themselves. They had left Toronto weeks before, en route to a bicentennial celebration at L'anse-aux-Meadows. The Gulf of St. Lawrence - not noted for calm waters - had kicked the hell out of them. They were now on their way back home, via St. John's and Boston.

Later, we split a bottle of wine. The evening turned mellow and conversations of the sea stretched deep into the night. I had a glorious time. It was good to be around fellow travelers, people who saw life through the same eyes, and when I eventually left to make camp, I left with the promised of a breakfast to snuggle up to.

The next morning was equal to the last; fog as thick as pea soup, and little to no wind. I was now getting use to it, and also to my compass. I was beginning to enjoy these rare close-up views of cliff rock. On clear days, my eyes tend to focus on the broader picture and less on the details. There were some spectacular caves and rock formations on this section of the coast and had it not been for the fog keeping me close to shore, I would surely have missed them.

At Sugarloaf, the fog mysteriously rolled back into the Atlantic. I still couldn't see the sun, but it got noticeably warmer. I was just starting to count my chickens and praise the weather gods, when a huge, billowing cloud pushed its way around a point, and visibility once again, dropped to zero. Immediately, the temperature plummeted and the seas fell quiet. Again, I found myself paddling in silence, only feet from cliffs. Coves and narrow inlets opened and closed in downdrafts of wind and once more, I found myself paddling more by sight than compass.

I was now closing in on Canada Bay. The last thing that I wanted, was to lose my bearings and find myself having to write a book based on a Trans-Atlantic crossing. At one point, a vertical face of rock loomed in front, a great tower of rock in twisting vapour. I had stopped, was checking my map, trying to pin-point my position, but it was hopeless. Coves were shallow, points of land shaved, and landmarks obliterated. I judged distances in yards, and time, by the sun's fuzzy halo above. I was halfway through a cup of coffee, drifting with my feet dangling over the sides into the water, rolling a homemade cigarette. Maybe it was the noise of the match striking or maybe it was the phosphorous light it made, but suddenly, my silence was shattered. Sea gulls peeled away from the rock face, above like snowflakes in a blizzard; hundreds of them, weaving, dive-bombing and zipping in and out of the fog in strobe lights of movement. I had disturbed them, big time, and they weren't too shy at calling me names.

Yet another window opened, then closed. The fog was teasing me, but this time it wasn't a joke. Maybe it was the cove's cornering wind that tore the fog apart at Canada Head, and then, maybe not. The fog opened just long enough for me to take a compass reading on Cape Daumalen's light beacon across the bay. The settlement of Englee was almost within my grasp, but as soon as I'd passed Canada Head, the fog choked out the views ahead.

For one hour, I strained my eyes to no avail; nothing, not a bird, boat or sign of life. I began second-guessing myself. Maybe my compass was broken, perhaps I was heading down the bay, or worse, still pointing out to sea. I had never been in fog so thick, or been so totally blinded, for so long. I was beginning to think the worst, that I'd need my passport, when I heard the sounds of licking water, then the slow putter of a speedboat's engine followed by its sighting. I hailed it, then lost it, then lost the sounds of land as well. The rocks couldn't have been ten paddle strokes away, but in which direction? I'd been so cocky, so sure the speedboat had come from the harbour, I'd just paddled towards it's wake, without thinking. I was so angry - not with the fog but with my own stupidity - that I almost broke my paddle, striking the kayak. Then I heard a door slam shut, engines start, then the sound of a car driving away.

When your eyes start focusing, it's like seeing a dam of colourful, liquid objects burst in front of you. What a beautiful sight. What an amazing place. Paddling into Englee, was like walking down a sidestreet. Every house had a wharf, and every wharf, a tied up speedboat or longliner. They looked like parked cars in driveways; a typical scene, straight out of suburbia. If ever I needed proof that a boat is as important, if not more, than a car on the coast, then here it was.

After so many hours of almost total silence, I now felt starved, hungry for human contact. I was paddling slowly, almost gliding. I'd heard the sounds of voices and was steering in their direction. I thought of calling out, then thought better of it. A surprise attack is always best. The surest way, my mother once said, to judge a man's personality, is to catch him with his trousers down. Were they drug smugglers? Separatists hatching a plot to blow up Parliament Buildings? Were they members of the Hells Angels? Was I possibly about to unwittingly eavesdrop on a murder confession? I was having the time of my life, just hanging back out of view, a silent witness. There was no train to catch and it wasn't as if I had a room to book, or even a meal to prepare. Englee is a town, by Newfoundland standards, bound to have a take-out restaurant. I waited until I could wait no more, then my eyes grasped onto their misty shapes and pulled the rest of me ashore.

........"Sees here, Dan's gone ta mainland. Mother's pretty upset. Knowt ta do round here......"

"Is this Englee?" God, I wish I'd taken a picture. They turned into my voice like two puppets on swivels.

"Bloody Hell!!!!!" They were gob-smacked.

"Eh, aren't ya the kayaker, the one paddling 'round island?"

"That's me.......but is this Englee?" I asked.

"Aye me boy.......E' paddle down here's and tie up. I'll get missis to put pot on."

"Proper thing". I didn't say it, but thought it. Could life get any better?

Who'd bet I'd get fog three days on the trot? If before starting, you'd given me odds of 5 to 1, I'd have taken them. Up until today, I had only seen fog about a dozen times. Not bad odds, when you consider that I'd been on the water for three months. And today, I couldn't have cared less. The shoreline, except for the scattered cove, was almost as straight as a ruler. I was still suffering a few aches and pains from White Bay's crossing, but nothing like the day after it. I still had rheumatic pinkies that needed prying apart before breakfast, but my grating wrists, tennis elbows, and sore knees, had healed themselves. Only my back, old hunch-back, wouldn't straightened without the sun. It still felt like red-hot needles, but other than that, Bernie felt OK.

Today, I got touchy-touchy, feely-feely with an iceberg. It was grounded, surrounded by growlers the size of grand pianos and an orchestra of birgy bits that crackled and popped. It had probably been pushed in by a northeasterly, then held fast by a falling tide. Some people view these as living history, evidence of the ice age, but to me, they are just another ingredient in the recipe that Newfoundland offers a traveler like myself.

They are a pleasant diversion, something my eyes can latch onto during a day's paddle. I had already counted over thirty so far, and August was the tail end of the season. Yearly, over one thousand icebergs visit the coastline of Newfoundland, and although I'd seen my fair share of them, down the Labrador coast on previous trips, I never tire of another look.

This one loomed out of the fog like an oceanliner. I could almost smell it. It wept constantly and the noise the waves made, lapping about its belly, reminded me of the rippled applause one sometimes hears at tennis matches. It wasn't huge - maybe three stories high, with the girth of a good size hockey rink - but then, everything looks larger than life when seen through mist.

The fog hung around all day, then lifted on cue as I approached the settlement of Conche.

I am a writer who likes to write from memory and don't like keeping a travel log. I work on the principle that if I can't remember the incident clearly, then it isn't worth writing about, but this trip was different. Having made up my mind to construct a website for school children and fellow kayakers to follow my progress, I now felt compelled to keep some kind of diary; a detailed analysis of local sea and wind conditions. I have already inserted some text that was posted on my website, and now, one I wrote in my log:

August 2nd
Conche to Fischot Island

Three days of fog have helped me. I feel fit and refreshed. The Conche Peninsula is amazing; sheer red cliffs, many birds nesting. The seas are calm and a slight tailbreeze helps.

After rounding the peninsula, I experienced cornering winds. Windy Point was windy, and the tickle at St. Julien Island was downright scary. The mountains have flattened and the whole coastline ahead looks like the sharp edges of broken glass. I am experiencing strong offshore breezes.

I couldn't find a suitable beach to camp on, so called into the small fishing community of Julien for a break. Invited for rabbit stew and homebrew. Could have stayed, but I wanted to camp under the stars. Tide and wind are now in conflict; waves are rafting all over the place. At Fischot Island, I made camp at its first beach - mistake.

After supper, I took a walk to the top of a hill, see its old, deserted settlement; lots of shelter, lots of good camping sites; ten more minutes paddling and would have made it.

God help me tomorrow. Hare Bay looks horrendous, full of surf.

That night, I took a sunset walk through Fischot's deserted settlement. It opened doors of bygone times; hearing children laughing, a mother's scold and men in rubbers. Some of the fishing stages had twisted and some yawned, as if buckled by earthquakes, sinking or rot from waves. I had walked amongst splintered wood and saw a brick chimney stack; the last remnants of a house, long since gone. Maybe it had been taken by some forgotten gale. A door left open to the elements, is like letting a fox loose in a chicken pen.

Newfoundland was once known as the baby basket of Canada. They left in droves during the 60's and plugged the holes caused by Canada's industrial growth. Countless Newfoundlanders now call places as far afield as Fort McMurray, Alberta, their home, and today, their children are the new technocrats of the oil industry. So many children, now grown up, piggybacked on my thoughts that night. The Newfoundland coast is freckled with these deserted outports, but I had never slept so close to one before, or felt such a crushing sense of loss.

Chapter: 18
Beware of the Clear Days

Imagine dropping a brick into a square bathtub. Now put in your favourite plastic boat and watch it being tossed around. Well, that's what it was like crossing Hare Bay on a clear day.

On a topographical map, Hare Bay looks deep but not wide, hilly but not mountainous, but such is the fantasy of maps. I never did check my bible, the Marine Weather Guide, or take into account that the tide was on the turn. Silly me! I thought the crossing would be easy. I even waited out an early morning wind before breaking camp. I'd paused until the seas were stretched taught and the torn clouds had billowed and healed. All looked calm when I started my traverse of the bay. Above, the sky was clearing and the sun was beating down. All looked well for the five mile crossing, but unbeknown to me, armies were forming below the sea's surface, readying themselves for attack. If only I had checked John's gospel to the Corinthians:

"Here sayeth the Lord, behold unto me. Beware of silent winds. Do not falleth into complacency, for behold the chariots of the devil, who at this very moment, are channeling, readying themselves to attack. Choppy seas are just around the corner and converging currents are of the devil's making..."

Of course, there's no such verse, but that day, it would have been a helpful guide.

If only.....how many times on this trip have I uttered those words? Waves didn't so much build, as explode from below, and to make matters worse, a sea was on. Towering sea swells peaked, broke and started to crest on the shoal waters ahead. I was concentrating, telescoping my vision towards the dark horn of Goose Cape, and hoping she wouldn't waver. I was blinkered to whatever was happening around me. When I am in real trouble, like that day, my brain seems to have the ability to process priorities in over-drive. Just like a baseball player who says he's in 'the zone', and who can see a baseball coming towards the plate, as if in slow motion and the size of a beach ball, so I can say, I was in a groove. At these times, my hips work on instinct. I don't have to see approaching waves to know when and where to brace. Sometimes my eyes focus ahead on faraway objects. They attach chords like moun-tain climbing belays of safety. On days like that, I could pad-dle with my eyes shut. I fervently believe that when I'm that frightened and pumped-up, that my body has the ability to make it own drugs, that it cannot only produce valium to calm my nerves, cocaine to heighten my sences, but also morphine to shut-down any physical pain. We all have these gifts deep within, an untapped resource that comes to our aid in times of enormous stress.

Note: It is a well known medical fact that during high adrenaline moments of "fight or flight", the body produces chemicals, endorphines, that act as energy and strength boosters and pain killers.

The seas around Lobster Point were huge. They lit up its face in clouds of spray, and their echoed report sounded like an artillery barrage. I cut corners entering St. Anthony's harbour below Fishing Point lighthouse. The reflective waves were enormous, sometimes clapping directly under my kayak and giving it wings. Rocks cruelly glinted, as I ran the gauntlet of surf, and what a buffeting it gave me! Again, I felt I'd reached a brink, but a final push through a wall of high breakers soon found me gliding out into a pool of glass calm water. In a matter of yards, the sea calmed and earli-er goosebumps smoothed. My day's paddle had only last-ed three and a half hours, but what a day and what a ride!

I was now beginning the last quarter of my trip, its final

chapter, and it couldn't have started on a better note. Two killer whales, breaching humpbacks and dolphins swimming under my kayak, had anointed me a lucky charm of spray. I was closing in on Cape Norman, Newfoundland's most northerly and barren point of land. Here, the scenery is treeless and windswept, its cliffs stunted, but with hills quilted in summer bloom and a shoreline abundant with beaches a pleasant change in scenery.

From St. Anthony, the current flowed north and with a tailbreeze to aid me, I made excellent progress. It was a typical midsummer day, hot and hazy and extremely humid. Now, with the exception of my fingers, I was as fit as a fiddle. While in St. Anthony, I'd visited its hospital. My wrists, although not as bad as before, still grated, but I was beginning to worry about my fingers. Not one, but three on each hand, had shut-down on me. Each morning, they required popping out. I didn't know whether it was from the onset of rheumatism or was caused by some tendon damage. The doctor had been pleasant, youthful, and thankfully, having paddled himself, had seen it before.

"It's caused by gripping your paddle tightly. It's not serious. You'll probably not see the end of it until you finish the trip."

I left him, feeling much relieved, and that morning, between paddle strokes, forced my fingers to loosen their grip.

I made Quirpon Harbour under gathering storm clouds, camped opposite its wharf, then cooked under what felt like a tropical downpour. I couldn't have asked for a better campsite. Nestled between two hillocks, on a carpet of moss, it soaked up the rain like a sponge. The rain continued until darkness fell, then a lightshow, equal to a prairie storm, started. For one hour, lightning flashed and thundered over my head, as if Star Wars had come to earth. Huge, billowing clouds and jagged streaks of lightning tore apart the sky and lit up the night in a spectacular exhibition of power.

I decided to take the next day off, to check all my equipment before the long haul back down the Northern Peninsula. On clear hot days, I enjoy playing hooky. I'd not taken many during this trip, but today, it felt good to relax into doing nothing. I did try. My gear got unpacked and shuffled around like a pack of playing cards on a table. I remember checking my food supply and even making a lame attempt at repairing my gas stove, but it hadn't taken long for the playing cards to collapse, and before noon, they lay scattered around my tent like fallen leaves. Work ethic and discipline flew out of the window with my mood. I just hadn't the energy, nor even the concentration to complete the smallest of tasks. I found myself staring out into the sea, and sat, for what seemed to be hours, watching the rhythmic lap of water on pebbles. It was intoxicating, or was it just boredom? Whatever it was, it did the trick. I slept the clock around.

Some rituals never change and the term, ritual, is an accurate description of cooking and eating in the confines of one's tent. To anyone unfamiliar with the process, it might appear that a religious ceremony was in process. I'd been lucky on this trip. Due to below average rainfall, the coastal mosquito had thinned to the point of extinction and black flies are no lovers of salt-laden sea air. I'd cooked my evening meals, more often than not, above roaring beach fires. This wasn't out of any need to conserve fuel supply. I simply prefer a roof of stars and an unrestricted view of the sea, over that of a canvas wall, but today, I couldn't even find a twig. The small beach below my camp, was as bare as a bone.

For the uninitiated, all actions while cooking inside one's tent, are done from a kneeling position, as if bent over on a prayer mat in a mosque. I always carry with me, a piece of plywood, a stable base for my stove. First, I boil a pan of water to make tea or coffee, then, whilst drinking it, prepare another pan of water for my main, one and only course of freeze-dried food. It's normally cooked within twenty minutes of being soaked in water. I have done it so many times,

I could do it blindfolded. Choclate bars are my dessert of choice and before bedding down, I'll wash and clean all my utensils, then make a thermos full of tea for the night.

Was it Erick the Red or Captain Cook?

I'm not an historian, but I do know that whoever settled in L'Anse-aux-Meadows, needed their heads examined. History tells us that the Vikings were a strong breed; fearless warriors and even better sailors, but what on earth possessed them to settle in one of Newfoundland's only coastal bogs, is anyone's guess. Maybe the term, Vineland, their word, not my mine, was for the abundant bake apples and partridge berries that grow in and around bogs, but why camp on top of one? Newfoundland wrote the book on sheltered, deep water anchorages, but this area is almost flat. Maybe the Vikings were just too tired to continue down the coast to St. Anthony, and the coastline of Labrador, with its high cliffs, sheltered bays and sandy beaches, only a stone's throw away, across the Straits. For whatever reason they chose this bay, it's not only been turned into a National Park, but UNESCO got into the act and it's now a World Heritage Site.

I couldn't escape the abundant B&B signs in Quirpon or its freshly painted houses and well paved roads. I'd been told the whole area around L'Anse-aux-Meadows had been given a facelift. Even from my kayak that day, en route to Cape Onion, I could make out its theme park and the numerous R.V's parked around its Orientation Centre. Not for one second, did I think of beaching and joining the crowd, but each to their own. Even the peculiar sight of a replica of a Viking sailboat, filled with both male and female sailors in traditional garb, and being towed by a longliner, couldn't waver my resolve to by-pass the sight. Of course, my decision wasn't only based on my dislike of being in and around tourists; the weather was glorious.

Sun, sun and more sun. The sea that morning looked like a silver disc. At Cape Onion, the Strait of Belle Isle yawned open, and the spectacular view of Belle Isle island's purple coloured rocks, viewed through a heat haze, was out of this world. It gave me the first view of Labrador's rocky coastline and the first taste of the Strait's strong head-currents.

What a strange day's paddle. Burnt Cape looked like an island, the throat of Pistolet Bay, due to its flat circumference, bottomless, and Shallow Bay looked anything but shallow. I had few landmarks to navigate by, and had it not been for a red tower at Cook's Harbour to aim for, and the distant lighthouse at Cape Norman to line up on, I could easily have become totally disoriented. Not until I'd attached myself to Schooner Island, did I know for certain, where I was......and on it I found my lucky feather.

That night, I camped on a beautiful beach near Whale Point. I built a fire out of broken lobster traps, cooked on it, then watched its embers die. I was gathering my thoughts for the long haul down the Northern Peninsula back to Corner Brook. Once I turned the corner at Cape Norman, I would be fighting not only the Strait's strong northeasterly sea currents, but also its prevailing winds. I knew that this section would offer few surprises. Its coastline is dotted with communities linked by a coastal road, and being twinned on the Strait's northern shoreline by Labrador, is sheltered from Atlantic storms. The only thing that punctured my good mood that night, was the sameness. There is nothing worse than having to paddle endlessly, from point to shallow point, knowing the elements are against you. There were few corners I could cut, almost no islands to escape behind, and daily, I could be seen from the road, but such is life.

Chapter: 19
Strait of Belle Isle

It was late morning by the time I rounded Cape Norman, into the sheltered water of the Strait of Belle Isle. I had woken early, into despair. My beach fire, washed by a rising tide, was just a stain in the sand, and my kayak was nowhere to be seen. The tide had risen almost to my tent, and the beach's newly glazed surface had erased all evidence that the kayak had been there. I was cursing everything, but mostly myself, then I saw it.

The tide had obviously caught it, not quite enough to carry it out, but enough to push it further along the beach. What a relief! I could easily have woken into my worst nightmare, had the tide risen a few more feet. All those days of toil wouldn't have added up to a hill of beans. Suddenly, the flood gates opened and I wept like a baby. In ten minutes, I vented off three months of anxiety. Since I was now in no fit state to leave, I climbed back into my sleeping bag and lost the rest of that morning to nerves.

The seas 'round Cape Norman were treacherous, not big, not rafting, clapping or filled with surf, but full of whirlpools and whiplashing back-eddies. This is not a place to go swimming or even to dip your toe, and once rounded, it didn't get any better. I now came under the influence of the Strait of Belle Isle. The force of its strong seaward current - aided by a falling tide and the forever flowing force of the Gulf of St. Lawrence - almost stopped me in my tracks. I ended up paddling at a crawling pace. It took me more than four hours to paddle ten miles to Boat Harbour. I just couldn't find a paddle rhythm, and without the help of a tail-breeze, would have packed it in, within spitting distance of the Cape itself.

The shoreline that I was now paddling, had changed dramatically since the cape. Cliffs had given way to shallow banks of rock, maybe twenty feet high, and sandy beaches were replaced by boulders. Just before Big Brook, I spotted a shipwreck, the second in two days, and I called it a day. Once again, my wrists were grating and my fingers, forever wet and cold, had lost their feelings. I was now becoming exhausted, more mentally than physically from my lack of progress, and a question was forming in my head, one that was now consuming my life ..... "When will the currents stop?"

That night, I jumped through another hoop. I was already dreading the next day's paddle. My early morning shock had reinforced how much this trip meant to me, and how much I wanted it to end successfully. Today's paddle had been an exercize in futility, and if I hadn't found some back-eddies close to shore, could have been soul destroying. I was keenly aware of how far I still had to go before the finish line. It doesn't seem to matter how many of these trips I've done before, I still had to jump through this endurance hoop. What was needed most at this stage of the trip, was a dose of hard paddling and to put up some big numbers.

I woke stiff and lethargic, but one hour's paddling undid those kinks. The sea was completely still, barely a ripple. Initially, it seemed oppressive. The view ahead, tapered into a heat haze, but by midmorning, shapes had darkened into points of land. It was a morning empty of life, devoid of colour and the seas were totally calm.

At Eddies Cove, the coastal road appeared and within no time, I had become a tourist attraction. Cars were honking and stopping and cameras were focusing in on my direction. Hands waved like windmills and invites to stop for a chat came thick and fast. Twice, I gave into coffee and biscuits, and one lady even insisted that she return home to fill my thermos.

At Lonesome Cove, it really started to blow. The ocean clouds were getting darker, emptying like leaky sieves and it was only a matter of time before they overtook me. I was now surfing, eating up the mileage. A strong breeze had turned into a stiff northeasterly, and whitecaps were forming in the Strait with steep, razor-sharp waves, in the shallows. I had not strayed more than a couple of hundred yards from the shore all day, and I'd already passed numerous campsite possibilities in the last few hours.

I was a driven man that day. My eyes were on the finish line, not on cloud formations, and by early evening, I was paddling in a full-blown storm. I had set my sights on paddling at least thirty miles, and thirty miles I paddled.

Beggars can't be choosers. That night found me camped out on a fishing stage. The heavens had opened and the wind howled. Any other night, I would have taken my tent down and found a more sheltered spot, but I was just too tired and wet to care. There was a distinct nip in the air. I had stripped, powdered myself dry, then slipped into my thermals. That evening I didn't even have the energy to cook a meal, simply made a thermos full of coffee, ate a handfull of Mars Bars, then turned in for the night.

I was woken at 5:30 am by two fishermen who had stopped by to pick up some gear before heading out. To see their complete lack of surprise at my presence, camped out on their stage, you would have thought that kayak sightings in Sandy Cove were a daily occurrence.

"Good day me b'y. Slept well?"

We exchanged the usual pleasantries and I thanked them for the use of their stage. They commented on the size of my kayak, then not for the first time on my trip, I was offered the run of a fishing shack.

"Bit chilly this morning. Woodya like a cuppa?"

Since I felt chilled to the bone, a second invitation wasn't needed. My wet suit was still damp and tent was saturated. I followed them on, creaking legs, up the stage to their shack. As usual, I accepted the invitation without embarrassment. It's always nice to wake into a breakfast invitation and more so, when it's cold and damp. It never ceases to amaze me, how kind and generous these people are. Life on the coast is simple; food is food, and shelter is shelter. Gourmet cooks may be as rare as indoor plumbing in a fishing shack, but that morning, I ate what they gave me, like an underfed seagull without thought of table manners. They'd lit the shack's stove for a brew-up, then without batting an eyelid, gave me half of their day's sandwiches of baloney and cheese, before leaving me to my own devices.

Even though I left on a full stomach that morning, wearing a dried wet suit and with a wave of goodwill, I still felt stiff and thick headed. My biorhythm must have been in a particularly low phase that morning or maybe it was due to a rising moon. Who knows, but after my hosts left, everything that could go wrong that morning, did. First, I snapped a tent pole in two and had to spend thirty minutes repairing it. Then, I stood on a nail and punctured my rubbers, and if I hadn't smelled burning fabric, I would have finished this trip without a sleeping bag. Lastly, to add insult to injury, I slipped on a rock, braced myself in some sand, and snapped my paddle. When things go wrong, they always seem to come in threes, so the saying goes. This time, there was an extra...... such is the life of a voyager.

That morning, the Strait of Belle Isle's northern shore offered up a fantastic view of Labrador's monstrous cliffs. Forteau Bay looked like the jaws of hell, and its Pointe Amour lighthouse, a huge phallic symbol of white. Across the Strait, the coastline was awash in a blue and purple haze, and no sooner had I rounded Anchor Point, when yet another view greeted my eyes. Further down the coast, half hidden behind a curtain of rain, and looking like a huge tidal wave of rock, was the Northern Peninsula's Long Range Mountains. At last, my eyes had something to aim for. I was less than one week's paddle away from the finish line. My tail now rose into the wind, and my earlier mishaps were flushed away. For once, I knew exactly where I would spend the night and who I'd spend it with, but never in my wildest dreams, did I think it would be so enjoyable.

Bird Cove may not be known to many people, aside from its local residents, but in the archaeological fraternity, it's known as a veritable treasure trove of human history. It's here, that the Maritime Archaic Indians made home, where the Dorset Eskimo hunted and where Portuguese sailors wintered. Over the years, this site had attracted both students and professors alike, and today, it would add a lone kayaker to its ever growing list of visitors.

There were two reasons why I was excited at the thought of staying in Bird Cove. The first and obvious, one is that it meant a night between clean sheets, but the main reason, the one that stoked the furnace that drove my paddles like pistons that day, was the thought of meeting its motley crew of workers. For over three months, I had held centre stage; the star attraction, but I knew that there, I would be lucky to even receive second billing. Work trumps entertainment on the coast, and after all, entertainment is all I could offer. Jobs are the number one issue in coastal communities; government make-work programs may be a dime-a-dozen, but to most people, it's a fact of life and not to be scoffed at. Most programs carry little prestige, don't offer much in the way of job security and have insignificant value outside the community where they're offered, but the place that I was paddling towards, was unique. Bird Cove's archaeological project not only offered the community summer employment for over thirty people, but with its forever expanding museum and orientation centre, may someday vie with L'Anse-aux-Meadows, as a premier league tourist attraction. Quite simply, employment means community survival, and that beats my sideshow anytime. I knew that under the roof of its program director, I could let my hair down with a certain anonymity. It's not that I mind being in the spotlight, but not day-in, day-out.

I'd met the project director, Tim, on the internet. He'd checked out my website, emailed me an invite, and last night, I'd called to confirm my arrival. All that was required of me, was to turn up; shower, laundry and food on the table, went unquestioned. I was in good spirits that day as I beached, and even better one hour later, drinking a glass of wine.

What a night; Tim, Mark, Dale, Miki, Latania and myself,

all ended up at the Legion for drinks. I'd not had so much fun in a long time, and even when some locals entered, like a junkyard of coiled wire, ready to pounce on the ladies, their nervous wobbly legs told a different story and before long, we were all playing darts.

In Miki, I found a kindred spirit. This girl had a voice built for calling in the wind and voicing strong opinions, and she wasn't shy at expressing them. Latonia was the goddess, Tim's right arm and poster girl. In her presence, I saw grown men shrink to the size of dolls. She was both rose petal and thorn, and you can guess which one I felt. Tim, the project director, was in a league of his own. He was the thinker, the boy doing a man's job, just one step away from bankruptcy, living from grant to grant, the hand-to-mouth existence that all researchers seem to live. They were all individuals in their own right. A motley crew, but a happy one.

The lame excuse of bad weather, was my ticket to stay on in Bird Cove for three days, but they didn't seem to mind. I am sure that to them, I was a happy diversion, and for me, their home turned into an oasis in the desert of travel.

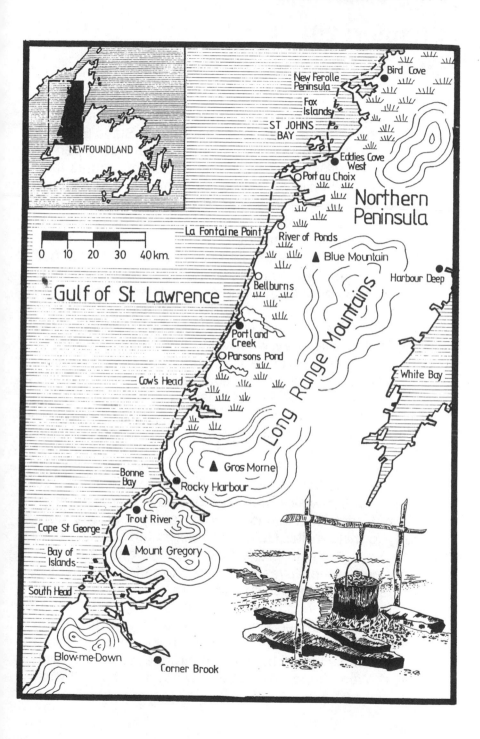

NEWFOUNDLAND

Bird Cove

New Ferolle
Peninsula

Fox
Islands

ST JOHNS
BAY

Eddies Cove
West

Port au Choix

Northern
Peninsula

La Fontaine Point

River of Ponds

▲ Blue Mountain

Harbour Deep

Gulf of St. Lawrence

0   10   20   30   40 km.

Bellburns

Port land
Creek

Parsons Pond

Cow's Head

White Bay

Long Range Mountains

▲ Gros Morne

Bonne
Bay

Rocky Harbour

Trout River

Cape St George

Bay of
Islands

▲ Mount Gregory

South Head

Blow-me-Down

Corner Brook

Chapter: 20
Gulf of St. Lawrence

I was now entering the Gulf of St. Lawrence. Labrador, on its northern shore, had last been seen at Blanc Sablon, and now, the Quebec Lower North Shore was tapering away into the distance. The strong, seaward currents that the Strait of Belle Isle generates, were history. From shore to shore, the Strait is less than twenty miles across, not enough distance to force up large waves, but the Gulf of St. Lawrence is a different story.

St. John Bay has taken its fair share of souls. It's not deep, not without islands to escape behind, but it's very susceptible to northeasterly and southwesterly winds.

The day I left Bird Cove started well enough. Autumn was in the air, but the sun was out, so the five mile crossing of St. Margaret Bay went without incident. I was now poised to island hop across St. John Bay. My plan was to cut in between Fox Islands, paddle between Whale Islands and camp the night on St. John Island, before completing the twenty mile crossing the next day.

The seas were seductively calm. I was resting on a sandbar under the shadow of Ferolle lighthouse. The clouds above, looked stretched and torn, not a good sign, but not an immediately bad one either. A northeasterly was blowing, but the waves weren't big. I saw very little chop, but now I knew that I was deluding myself. Waves were already forming in the Gulf. I had estimated it would take me an hour, tops, to make Fox Islands; long enough, I thought before the waves would start to raft. I was just too lazy, too focus on the finish line, to rein myself in. My gut said, stay, but my head said, go for it.

The wind picked up slowly and steadily and so did the waves. My inner alarm system was ringing, but I was in a different world. Hadn't I been out in stronger seas? On colder days? Weren't the views ahead worth the effort? It wasn't until a wave came from nowhere and swamped me, that my bubble burst. Not only were the waves rising above my head, but curling. I'd drifted over shoal. It was so shallow in the waves' trough, I could see rocks below. I was in trouble, big trouble, and I still had some distance to go.

Yet another wave swamped me, then another. I could have kicked myself. I dug in and sprinted. I paddled like the devil for twenty minutes, bracing on instinct, crashing into and through waves, and sometimes getting slapped by chest-high walls of water. Once again, I never really felt in danger. I allowed my eyes to latch onto a sandbar, then reeled myself up to it.

I landed close to some cabins, pulled my kayak up the sandy beach, then walked up a rise of land to gain a better view.

Wow!! At that moment, I couldn't have cared less about the sea. I wasn't looking out into the gulf, or inland towards the mountains, but towards a golden carpet of bake apples; thousands of them, and ripe for the picking.

To understand my love of bake apples and bake apple cheesecake in particular, I have to take the reader back to my first trip in Labrador and my first slice of bake apple cheesecake. Bake apples are not so much a unique taste, as a journey. They only flourish in subarctic regions. I'd heard of children selling them by the bucketfulls on the Northern Peninsula roadside. Some Newfies call them liquid gold. Their suntans set them apart. I do believe, given the choice, they would gladly be adopted as local currency. Whether cooked or eaten freshly picked, it's impossible to take away their crunch. It's the pip that catches between your teeth, that makes them special, and the flavour of bittersweet has always sent my taste buds crazy. I am what is called a bake apple junkie. I could eat bake apple jam for breakfast, bake apple pie for dinner and crunchy bake apple squares for supper, but bake apple cheesecake is my favourite, and this, I could eat from dawn to dusk. But once again, I'm heading off on a tangent, so let's get back to the rest of my island experience.

There are two types of R & R; the one that allows you to sleep the hours away, totally undisturbed by man or beast, and the one that allows you to let your hair down, as in Bird Cove. Fox Island turned in to be the former.

Now, close your eyes and imagine a deserted island. You have a room with a view, a radio, a good book, a warm bed and a vivid imagination to curl up with. I could not have found a better place to wait out a storm.

For three days, a strong southwesterly wind kept me pinned to the land, but I didn't care. I was in heaven. I'd found a cabin door open; it had a library, a radio and a soft bed to lie on. The island's head was carpeted from one end to the other, in bake apples. The wind kept the flies away, and I could work on an all-round suntan while picking, without fear of being spotted or bitten. I woke every morning to the velvet tones of CBC's Michael Enright, and every evening, was tucked into bed by Kurt Vonnegut's coptic humour, but all good things come to an end, and it wasn't the weather that finally drew me back onto the sea, but one of my vices....

On the second morning, I rose with the sun. I wanted an early start, but when I peered out of the window, a second glance wasn't needed to tell me that I wasn't going anywhere that day. The sky was grey, light rain streaked across the window and white-crested waves scarred the bay. By 9:00 am, I had as much sleep as I wanted and got up, but the day passed slowly. I was now rationing my water, eating only peanut butter, and was down to smoking dried tea leaves from used tea bags. The weather forecast was tuned in at every opportunity and I'd paced back and forth so many times from window to door, that I had almost worn out a groove. I was willing the weather to change and when suddenly, the wind died, I almost wet myself with excitement. But this is Newfoundland, the land of wind and rain, so no sooner had I started to pack, when it returned with a vengeance.

It's at times like these, that I feel I'm being punished for something that I don't deserve, and being trapped within four walls, only makes it worse. These are the times when I turn to drink, the great anaesthetizer, my back shelf of last resort, and a stupid decision. Alcohol would only increase my thirst, but I didn't care. I left the shack, went straight for my kayak, dug out my emergency kit and returned with the brandy.

Solitary drinking is a dangerous thing. You can drink all night and not even feel the remotest sense of intoxication, but when you rise, you discover that while your head feels clear enough, your legs have decided to revert to baby walking. Clumsy isn't the word. Let's just say I was uncoordinated, took more time than usual to pack away, but I did leave.

When I look back at how I felt that morning, I do believe I would have left in a gale. My throat was not only parched and craved water, but even worse, my body was suffering mega withdrawal symptoms from lack of nicotine. Seriously, the conditions didn't look all that bad. Maybe, and I do mean maybe, if I would have had some tobacco and lots of water, I may have waited out another day, but that's only a maybe. I'd clear-cut the bake apples, spilled my imagination over half a dozen letters and run out of things to do. The radio had called for moderate winds and although the bay was full of lop, it was obviously fighting a falling tide. In a few hours, it would turn and then the seas would calm. I left on this principle of tide and wind, and kept my fingers crossed that I was right.

I packed quickly and slipped out past breakwaters, into the open sea. The early morning swell from northwest, now changed direction with the wind. It caught me by surprise, picked up in force, then started funnelling between St. John Island and the mainland. I was in a dreadful state. The seas were whiplashing around me, waves were rafting, and the windborne surf was blinding. So close, yet so far away. Not for the first time on this trip, did I say a silent prayer. Not that it helped, but I did eventually gain a toehold.

Was I ever glad to get ashore; to be invited for coffee and biscuits, and have my first cigarette in two days. Thank God for small mercies, for what happened next, was more than I deserved. Of course, the coffee stretched into an evening meal and then, to a night between clean sheets.

Everything, and I do mean everything, from the hunchback to my grating wrists returned. The wind and surf had drained me and within minutes of eating a meal of fried cod, I was ready to hit the sack.

I woke bright and early. Catherine Lawless had made a delicious breakfast and her husband, had already checked the weather forecast for me. A good night's sleep had done a world of good. I was back to my perky self, bursting with energy, and I hit the water, immediately striking a rhythm. Once again, Newfoundland was smiling on me. The sun beat down all morning and the sea was becalmed.

A longliner putted by, in a blaze of colour, with a wake like the hem of a slip, showing beneath it. It was beautiful; vivid red with blue trim in a bleached sky. I snapped its picture, filed it in memory, then watched as it turned in the direction of Port-au-Choix.

What a difference a point makes. I rounded Pointe Riche Peninsula and immediately lost the horizon. Vapour clouds were twisting and turning in a soupbowl of fog. I was resting at the point, trying to get my bearings across Ingornachoix Bay. Port Saunders was nowhere in sight. I could still see the two towering peaks of the High Lands of St. John, to the west and the distant Long Range Mountains to the south, but the seas I was paddling, were mere shadows of themselves. I sat watching yet another longliner. The sun lit it up as it punctured the fog like a sparkler, then it arced around the point until the only evidence she existed, were her pulsating engines. Even though the fog banks didn't intimidate me, I wasn't enthusiastic at paddling blindly across the bay. Port Saunders is a busy harbour and who knows how many boats were now in its waters? I tried to skirt it as much as I could. Two miles out, the fog had thinned into islands of vapour, and three miles out, it was as clear as day, but still all but the coastal mountains were hidden.

I paddled in silence for two hours, then suddenly a stallion of steel exploded out of the gloom. I could hardly believe my eyes. A jetboat, more fitted for the expensive waters around Toronto, reared up in front of me; a water-borne muscle-car, complete with spotlights and blaring disco, a hotrod, driven by the hormonally imbalanced and propelled by gasoline. Who's kidding who? And when he stalled, making a tight turn, I almost blew a fuse, laughing.

By noon, it had started to drizzle close to shore, but after it finished, out came the sun. I was taking a break at River of Ponds. I was sitting down on a park bench, when a moose appeared. It looked more surprised than me. It grunted, waved its many pointed antlers in my direction, then dissappearing back into the bush.

They say there are as many moose as people on the

Rock, and I'd half expected to see one on this trip, but never within a stone's throw of a road. Then I saw another, then another. I ended up counting six, grazing by the side of the road and one showlder deep in slew water. Taking a picture never entered my head. It was like going to the butcher's shop. All I could think of was, "When does the hunting season start?" and I'm not even a hunter.

Again, I found myself paddling under the watchful eyes of drivers, cameras pointing and firing in my direction. One even followed me, for what felt like hours, with his family in tow, before speeding off to Bellburns, where he reappeared the next day on a beach.

Highway 430 is married to the coast, follows it like a tracer, and was hardly ever out of view. It brought with it, not only an alien noise and beady eyes, but also its drivers' garbage. It's easy to see life's underbelly when you're on the road, when you are passing through someone else's back garden. The corroded metal of civilization lie in every outport, high and dry, like dirty underwear. You can see everything from rusty draggers, to rotten dorys, to ancient ribcages, sinking into sand. These coastal communities are littered with the broken government promises of Newfoundland's Fisheries, but it's not until the roads touch a shoreline, that you see the human wastebin of everyday life. I had already lost count of discarded kitchen units, rusty stoves jammed between rocks, and even an open fridge, lodged in sand, halfway down a cliff. People are people, and garbage is garbage. I guess it's safer to drop-off garbage on common land than on your own. If you look on the bright side, today's garbage is tomorrow's archeological find, evidence that life existed before the fisheries collapsed. So far, I'd found a fortune in empty beer bottles. Even on the coast's most isolated shores, traces of human activity are never far away; torn fishing nets, broken lobster traps, empty plastic bottles, boat parts, even a whole speedboat, bleached and blistered, left upside-down on the shore, and this doesn't even start scratching the surface of broken wood and rusty cans.....

C'est la vie. It's life on the coast, and I'd gladly accept twice the amount of garbage if it would help to bring the fish back. It is easy to forget that these waters were once work yards, not playgrounds for kayakers like myself. Garbage, if left, will accumulate and attract more, like flies to cow chit, and the last thing a tourist wants to trip over, is someone else's cast-offs.

Tonight's camp would have been unimaginable at the beginning of the trip, but my roll downhill to the finish line, was gaining momentum. I was paddling longer into the day, passing up ideal campsites and picturesque fishing communities, for the sake of mileage. I was in cruise control, or was it overdrive?

I have no idea where I camped that night. I had seen a crack in low-lying cliffs, dragged my kayak above the tide line, then made camp between some rather weak looking trees on its lip. In no fit state to go on, my tanks were empty. The sun was still high in the sky, but carried little heat. The trees' inland tilt that must surely have been caused by winter storms, gave them the look of a set of bent candles. The wind blew the day away and most of the night. Tent pegs popped out at regular intervals, like rivets under pressure, and in the morning, my tent's tilt matched that of the trees.

Chapter: 21
Long Range Mountains

What a slippery slope I woke on! The sky surged with a storm and even when it brightened, the distant sun only half stared through the racing clouds. It didn't look promising but neither did my campsite, and it only took a few spits of rain to mobilize me into action. I broke camp at break-neck speed, then hid behind some bushes to heat up some water for my thermos.

Though the Long Range Mountains were impressive, towering above my horizon, the constant view to my left, of the unchanging, low-lying cliffs of sand and, rock was monotonous. To keep my spirits up that morning, and away from the storm clouds behind, I lost myself to my favourite menus. One minute, I would be in Mysore, India sitting down in Jinja's Spice Kitchen, eating one of his specialty hot rice plate dinners and drinking a cool lassi made out of creamy yogurt. Next, I'd find myself in the Rising Moon on Lamu Island, Kenya, eating a freshly made sugar-fried mandazi. My mother's staple of Yorkshire pudding melted before my eyes, and a bag filled with fish and chips had me drooling. Since starting out on this trip, I'd eaten a smorgasbord of dishes, especially the ones with main ingredients of wild game. I'd indulged in platefulls of moose and caribou, and on more than one occasion, pickled rabbit. I'd eaten sea life as varied as cod, halibut, squid, caplin, skate, trout, salmon, flounder, lobster, mussels, crab, shrimp and scallops served in a rich garlic sauce. I enjoyed varieties of duck, grouse and pickled partridge. My staple diet has always come with mountains of potatoes, garden grown carrots, turnip, cabbage and beets. It was berry time and bake apples now lined dried-out bogs, like honey drops. There had been late wild strawberries, cranberries and even the scattered blueberry. I'd not wanted for food on this trip, and I was sure I'd put on more weight than I'd lost.

I arrived in Bellburns, frothing at the mouth like a rabid dog. I was ravenous, and no sooner had I beached, when I took off like a bloodhound in search of a store. I'd hit the wall. I hadn't eaten a choclate bar in two days, and wanted a fix. When I asked the lady, behind the counter for some Mars Bars, she replied, "How many luv?" I asked her how many she'd got, but before she could reply, said, "I'll take the lot." I bought six Mars Bars, two Kitkats and a Snickers. They weren't eaten all at once, but I sure made a dent in them, before leaving.

When the wind blows, it sure blows, and when it's carrying rain, it carries a punch. I lost sight of Bellburns to an horrendous downpour; not the heavy type that bubbles and boils in the sea, but the type that atomizes into fine mist, erases views like a snow blizzard, and whistles around your ears like a whining child. I had been forewarned by the store keeper in Bellburns, of a coming gale. This was its front, its first gear, and it would crank-up notches of force during the rest of the day.

I was now being pushed along at a sprinter's pace. It was risky, but I knew that every mile put in, this late in the game, would feel like two less miles to paddle. I had not expected tailwinds down the Northern Peninsula, but then, I'd not expected summer to end so quickly. My weather guide still called for southwesterlies, but since turning the corner at Cape Norman, the winds had been half and half. Who knew when it would make an about turn and blow in my face?

My windblown progress went from a sprint, to a crawl, to a snail's pace, in less than sixty minutes. The wind died, the skies opened and the sun came out..... then, wouldn't you know, the wind swung around 180 degrees and started to blow again. My energy banks drained like a leaky cup. I wasn't searching for a beautiful, shady beach that afternoon to camp on, but when I did find one, I felt I deserved it.

The cove was shallow, but sheltered; close enough to the community of Portland Creek to use its store, but far enough away to deter most unwanted visitors. It didn't take long to erect my tent, but it also didn't take long for the windborne sand to almost bury it.

There is no disappointment as painful as the fall that comes from great expectations, and that's how I felt, in the certain knowledge that I would be stormbound for at least two more days.

"Are you sure?" I was almost pleading with the store's owner, hoping another one of his customers would offer me a different opinion. "No, me b'y. When she blows like this; they'll be nowat be any boat owta here. Seas pretty rough and forecast is for much of same for next few days."

I sighed like a young child. So close, but no cigar. I could almost taste the finish line, but it was only momentary. The bell rang as the door opened, and I turned to face the village joker.

"By the Lord Jesus b'y. Are you the kayaker that's going round the Rock?"

"Aye, that's me," I replied.

"Ya cum all that way in a little boat....tha's crazy!"

A week, ago his words may have irritated me, but today, they were not only light relief, but all the excuse I needed to pass the day away. Most local stores not only dispense groceries, act as agents for Canada Post, but their owners are experienced psychotherapists. Within minutes, all three of us were sitting down, surrounded by open cartons, smoking and putting the world, if not my sex life, to rights.

"Where's ya woman?"

Well that was a new one.

"As ya queer or what me b'y? I thought all ya left footers, sorry, I mean Catholics, were breeders."

There are two topics all real men should not talk about, politics and religion, and I'd broken this golden rule when I'd asked them what the denomination of their church was. It's common knowledge in Europe, that there are two houses, no matter what economic ups and downs a community may go through, that will outlast everything else; the pub and the church, or in Newfoundland terms; the Legion and the

Ministry. Most of Newfoundland's history has either been written by, or through the eyes of its doctors, ministers, teachers or Mounted Police, and I put travelers in this category as well. It's easier sometimes, to view life from the outside looking in. I think that's why some many books on Newfoundland have been penned by these people. Religion is as good as any litmus test, when it comes to building a picture of life on the coast, and it was the only reason I brought it up that day. Each community has a character unto its own, whether moulded by the resource that it's built on or adjacent to, and for me, the outward expression of this character, is reflected in the abundance of its denominations. At last count, and they are still rising, I've encountered Presbyterian, Pentecostal, Methodist, Church of England, Evangelical, Baptist, Seven Day Adventist, Salvation Army and the all-powerful Catholic Church. Statues of the Virgin Mary, crosses of Christ and pictures of Saints may have been succeeded by Michael Jackson and Pink Floyd, but they are still a potent force in family life. I've heard some beautiful choirs at practice on this trip, listened to organ music on more than one occasion, and I will never forget Johnny Cash.

Of course Catholics, especially Irish Catholics, are supposed to be sinners - after all, we have the confessional - and saying three Hail Mary's can be a penance for many sins. This man wasn't so much questioning my manhood, but my saintliness. What a great conversation we had. It filled in a blank day, but sadly, didn't take away the wind.

Portland Creek, like so many coastal communities on the Peninsula is neither nestled behind points of land, down at the bottom of their sheltered armpit nor stuck to rocks, as if by magic. This compact little community lies at the southern end of a two mile sandy beach. I would describe it as prim and perfect. It didn't so much unravel around a central point such as a wharf, church, or school, as stretched around a road. Tended gardens were the size of prayer rugs, and scrap yards of recycled parts lay like overgrown cemeteries around most people's homes, but you don't judge a book by its cover.

I normally judge communities by their stores. This one was compact, but stocked like a warehouse, a mini Wal-Mart, with cartons cut open and contents displayed; haphazard enough to confuse an outsider like myself, but interesting enough to tease the locals. I'd seen my fair share in the last three months, and this one, I rated as above average.

Outside, the wind screamed and back on the beach, it felt like walking in a sandstorm. I had plenty of time that afternoon, to reflect on my trip, especially on the people I'd met. Soon, names were rattling in my head like dried bones. I began to wonder just how far I would have gone without their help. Time would blur my memory and soon, details would be lost, but I was also certain that the overall picture would never disappear. From the outset of this trip, I allowed the people I met, rather than the elements, to dictate where my head would rest. Sometimes, it had been hard keeping to this rhythm; one night camped under the stars and the next, between clean sheets. Sometimes, it left me a little punch-drunk. It can be both seductive and repellent, when you become public property, but still, I wouldn't have changed it for the world.

Later that day, a school teacher dropped by my camp. One thing led to another, and later that day, using his home internet access, I posted these thoughts on my website:

August 18th
The Long Yawn:
There was a time when I couldn't buy a southwest wind for love or money. Now, when I just don't want them, I can't get rid of them.

For two months, the weather has been inconsistent to say the least, but ever since I turned the corner at Cape Norman and started my long paddle south, these long-lost southwest winds have suddenly turned up at my doorstep. With the exception of two days, I have woken to find myself facing a day's paddle into a headwind, and coupled with the fact that the sea current on the Strait of Belle Isle travels north, YUK!!!

These southwest winds are like a monkey on my back, but one thing is in my favour, I have no more big bays to cross. From here on in, I can damn well walk the shoreline and pull my kayak home. I am over two weeks ahead of schedule, with time to spare, and I am using it. I must have stopped and visited nearly all the penninsula's northern outports. If I don't stay the night in one, at least I take a pit-stop and walk their streets. People now speak of me as the Kayak Man, the guy my brother saw yesterday, or, who stayed with my uncle last night in....

This trip won't go down as my fastest, longest, hardest, or the one where I met the girl of my dreams, but oh, what a story it will make: "Around the Rock in a Bad Mood, the weather was brutal but the hospitality, fantastic."

Today, the weather seems hell-bent on finishing the summer as it started, in a bad mood. A gale warning has been in effect for the last two days and I've been pinned to my tent. Since starting this final leg, I have spent five days stormbound and two delayed due to bad behaviour, ha! It is like Newfoundland doesn't want me to leave.

As I write, I have everything except the kitchen sink in my tent, to anchor it down. The wind is relentless and the sound of sand, peppering the tent, has a song all its own, but what is new?

I am camped on a beautiful beach with an amazing backdrop of dunes and a view of ocean surf, pounding the beach only yards away. Only a fifteen minute walk from Portland Creek, I have become a regular visitor at its store. I haven't spent much money on this trip, so I have been indulging myself by polishing off all their Mars Bars and now, I am into their Snickers. I have been buying pre-made sub sandwiches and chips galore. This is getting me ready for the real world; preparing my stomach for all the junk food it offers. I am only four good days' paddling away from Corner Brook, yet it seems like only yesterday, I said good-bye to Sept-Isle, my apartment and my friends.

Chapter: 22
What goes around comes around

The naked essence of Gros Morne, lightly coated in brown moss and half hidden behind a blue morning haze, underscores better than any other sight, what Newfoundland stands for; "Come hell or high water, we're not going to budge." Jutting out like a defiant chin against the elements, with a dusting of purple on its flat head, it looked every inch the "Rock" that Newfoundland is fondly called. You can keep the jagged peaks of the Rockies; they're still growing and haven't paid their dues. The Himalayas are too white, distant and unobtainable for my liking. The Alps are too picturesque and the Piranese, too road friendly. I've seen them all, but Gros Morne, seen on a wild day under brooding clouds, beats the lot. This mountain may have been spawned by a volcano, etched by glaciers, but it's the elements of wind, rain and snow that have moulded its character. Gros Morne isn't a pretty sight, but it dominates the landscape that it stands on, like no other mountain I've ever seen. Sure, the world is full of mountains, almost all bigger, but none that can reflect more about the people that live in its shadows, and by that, I mean all Newfoundlanders. I've seen it many times and it's never diminished in my eyes, especially on the morning I paddled into Cow Head.

I'd been struggling all day, against a moderate headwind. It had worn me down physically, but not mentally. Gros Morne had fed my spirits. I had seen it through mist, and felt in rain and angry clouds, what she had experienced through a millennia of storms. She watched over my progress that day, like a protective mother. I latched onto her ramparts and pulled at her hem for eight hours. I doubt if I covered twenty miles that day, and without this mountain in front, doubt if I would have made ten. After three days of sand storms in Portland Creek, the nights camped on its beach, had become unbearable. The winds that morning, were still coming out of the southwest and the seas were still choppy, but enough was enough.

Cow Head looked strangely abandoned; a town with its back to the sea, because you don't turn your back on Gros Morne. As with almost all fishing communities, it had declined in recent years. It had gone from an all-year-round settlement, to a summer one, and now, only a scattered few families remained. In recent years, it has gone through a renaissance. Artisans have displaced fishermen and it was easy to see why. Connected by a causeway to the mainland, its views of the Long Range Mountains, Gros Morne in particular, were worth the price of home purchase and renovation. The houses ranged from dilapidated to gentrified. Paint peeled from most houses, like flaking skin, whilst others, painted in traditional reds, blues, purples and greens, were picture-perfect.

That evening, I watched a Gulf sunset, sitting down with a rum and coke, in a deck-chair on a yacht built for two. How many times have Newfoundlanders embraced me and my trip? I've lost count.

Before turning in, I went for a walk. Gros Morne was an important landmark. I was now on the finishing straight. Time and the weather were no longer a major factor to consider, only a nuisance. With a bit of luck, the cliffs around Bonne Bay would damper any more winds, and once past Trout River, I knew, from experience, to expect a tailwind. If the gods were smiling, I could be back at Bob's, with my feet up, in three days, maybe even two. That night, I slept like a baby. I felt fit and confident, and just to underline it, finished off the last of my brandy.

What a tease! The predawn weather forecast called for expectations of good weather - sounded to me, a little like waiting for an old girlfriend at the steps of the local cinema. I knew she'd turn up sometime, but probably later rather than sooner.

I woke into a beautiful day; fresh, crisp and breezy. The wind had swung around during the night, and now came from the east. It started as an offshore breeze, but turned southerly as the day progressed. By noon, pushed along by its tailwind, I was paddling at a jogger's pace. I had the bit between my teeth, and come hell or high water, I had every intention of making Rocky Harbour that night. The day went without incident. I owned the sea. In fact, since Notre Dame Bay, I'd only seen the scattered speedboat. The lobster fishing season had ended weeks before and the coastal waters were now empty of traffic. I still saw the occasional longliner, but nearly always distant, never close up. My days were ones of solitude. I had initially missed my encounters with fishermen, but now, being alone was just a fact of life.

Autumn was in the air. Once again, I found myself between seasons. Only the week before, I was stripped and basking in the heat. Now, I half expected to wake up into frost.

I covered over thirty miles none-stop that day, and what breaks I took, were in my kayak, that is, until I reached the mouth of Bonne Bay.

The seas around Lobster Cove, below its lighthouse, were roaring. The tide was falling, rafting in places and creating whirlpools of motion in others. Rocky Harbour was in full view, less than a mile away, on the cove's southern shore. After six hours in the kayak, I needed a rest, and this seemed the perfect spot. I lodged my kayak between rocks, took out my thermos and drank the remaining mouthfuls of coffee that were left. I was probably sitting down on the rocks for less than ten minutes, but when I tried to stand, my back locked.

I was in shock. The last time this happened, I ended up bedridden for days. I literally had to crawl my way back to the kayak. I couldn't stay where I was. The point below the lighthouse was littered in boulders, and an unpenetrable line of storm logs, knotted the cliff's face. Somehow, I managed to pour myself into the kayak, then turtle my way off a ledge and between two rocks. For ten minutes, I willed myself into open water, then a rough wave tipped me. Instinctively, I turned into the wave and leaned into it with my paddle, then it happened.

Holy Chit ....it felt like someone had plunged a white-hot dagger between my shoulders. I was a little comatose, but it had done the trick. The knot my back muscles had got themselves into, unknotted, the moment my arm had risen above my shoulder. For sure, it frightened the living daylights out of me and led to a sleepless night, but the next morning, I felt none the worse for the experience.

The scenes from Cow Head to Rocky Harbour had been magnificent. The high, misty steps of Gros Morne, and the constantly changing, undulating coastline, with its shallow coves, and quiet, natural harbours, had been great, but they were nothing compared to today's experience around Bonne Bay.

Because of June's windy weather, I never did get up close and personal with the Southern Shore's coastline. I'd viewed its towering cliffs from a distance, and could only imagine paddling point to point across its fjord-like inlets, but today, I rectified this injustice.

Bonne, roughly translated from French, to English means happy, jolly even, but Bonne Bay, traversed under dark, threatening clouds, was downright scary. Just the memory of crossing its menacing mouth from Rocky Harbour to Wester Head, gives me goose-bumps. This glacier-scarred fjord of sheer cliffs, was one of my highlights, and when it started to crackle with thunder, an absolute thrill.

I couldn't have asked for a better day, or a tougher test from the seas. This was the Newfoundland I had started with, and this was the Newfoundland I wanted to finish with; rock, rock and more rock; wind, wind and more wind - a fitting tribute to complete the circle. In short, "what goes around comes around."

The wind was cornering, coming from the south and

compressing against the high cliff walls around the bay. That day, it threw everything against me. Cliffs echoed to the sounds of crashing waves and swells came at me from every direction. I got broadsided by waves from the Gulf, encountered reflected waves from the cliffs and experienced strange ones under the influence of underwater sunkers. I was having the time of my life, and it only got better.

Just before Trout River, the seas really tested me. Whipped-up by a strong southwesterly, their full force facing me around a point, they gave me the ride of the trip. There were no escape routes. To turn 'round and go back was never an option, and to skirt them this late in the game, felt downright cowardly. I wanted to meet them head-on, and I did. Crests, like cruel smiles, roared towards me and troughs as deep as valleys, opened, ready to suck me down. My kayak rose and fell with sickening thuds. My map case, attached by a chord that had held tight for over three months, snapped, and was instantly lost to the sea. I knew that Trout River was close, but in these conditions, not close enough, but that's how it should be when you're being tested, especially today, within shooting distance of Corner Brook.

Over the months and weeks of paddling, my eyes had become finaly tuned to searching for landmarks; spotting buoys between waves and half hidden sunkers. Everything on the coast told a story, the shape of a bay, or a crooked point. Silhouettes of hills denote downdrafts, sandbars, hidden riptides, and who can forget her capes, those defiant ramparts of rock that set Newfoundland apart from the rest of Canada? I was accustomed to looking at manmade features, like towers, antennas and oil storage tanks, not as blights on the landscape, but beacons of direction. I had become sensitive to subtle changes; a chill in the air, or dampness, currents that slow or accelerate one's progress, or when fog drops its grey blanket over the sea. Sometimes, all these clues seem out of sync with your chart, not to be found when expected. That's when you start feeling very small on that great big sea. Just like today; I knew I was within spitting distance of Trout River, but how far can one spit before one runs out of spittle? Twice, I rounded nipple points of land, and came up empty; then I heard it.

UHHHHHHH........UHHHHHHHH

It was a groaning harbour buoy and right on cue.

It's easy to look back now and say,"You're crazy boy!" but everyone likes to push the envelope now and again. Sure, I was relieved to see the buoy and turn into its sheltered harbour, but would the smiling faces at the wharf, those same faces, look at me differently, had I arrived in glass calm conditions? Afterall, don't all fishermen have stories, weather-beaten faces and callouses on their hands? I didn't enter the harbour with an Eskimo roll or an attitude of check me, "See what I've done." I was as tight as a drum, my lips were sealed and my nerves were dancing. I hardly had the energy to stand straight, let alone take a bow. The first few questions that flew my way - nearly always about my kayak - were like trying to understand gibberish; too long, too scientific and worse still, attached to hands that moved too quickly. It's at these moments, when I am sinking in questions that I can't answer, and am too exhausted to escape, that my guiding angel appears. I could bank on it. Someone always steps forward from the crowd, the eye in the hurricane, and rescues me. It is not so much what they say, but their body language, that propels their words forward in circles of hypnotic sound. I quite literally submit to whatever they have in mind. Today's shelter was a tool shed, no big deal, but just what the doctor ordered; a roof over my head and then food in my belly. How many times have I written that?

Chapter: 23
Welcome Home

"Ground Control to Major Tom."

I was in heaven, singing all my favourite songs and stroking the water with the same rhythms. A better finishing morning couldn't have been planned. The sky was crystal clear, and I had a tailwind. I still had to paddle over forty miles, but I couldn't have scripted my last day any better. Cape St. George was awesome, like looking down from the edge of the world. Surely it was sights like this, the ones that seem to slip away from you into infinity, the ones that give you vertigo, that spawned the theory that the world is flat, and it only got better.

The Bay of Islands, viewed from the foot of Mount St. Gregory, looked like Monument Valley in water, but it wasn't the islands' immense rock formations that my eyes rested on. I was edgy, searching the horizon for something else, something manmade, something, I hadn't seen in 94 days, and it wasn't until I traversed around the back of The Pillars and was pointing south down the bay towards Corner Brook, that I saw it. The beacon light at South Head.... still blinking out the same old message, but this time its translation read.... WELCOME HOME.

There comes a time in any trip when enough is enough and to accept any more would be overkill. My last day in the saddle turned into a glorious day of self indulgence. It was as though I had been preparing myself for over three months for this very moment. That day belonged to my ego. You see, I was 51, and knew my days of long distance travel were numbered, at least at this level. I wanted one last shot at the big time. One last shot at putting in some heavy duty mileage before hanging up my paddles, and today, the weather was completely in my favour.

It's hard to imagine the thoughts that one has on the last day of a trip. A good woman and good food immediately come to mind, but today, all my thoughts were on the finish line, and I paddled to the very limit, of my endurance.

I made Corner Brook under the cover of darkness. I had covered well over forty miles in twelve hours. In short, I felt great; great to be alive, feeling fit, and glad the trip was over.